Presented to

From

Date

Life Promises for Eternity

LIFE PROMISES

for ETERNITY

inspirational thoughts and verses

RANDY
ALCORN

Tyndale House Publishers, Inc. • Carol Stream, Illinois

Visit Tyndale online at www.tyndale.com.

TYNDALE and Tyndale's quill logo are registered trademarks of Tyndale House Publishers, Inc.

Life Promises for Eternity

Library of Congress Cataloging-in-Publication Data

Alcorn, Randy C.
　　Life promises for eternity / Randy Alcorn.
　　　　p. cm.
　　Includes bibliographical references (p.　　) and index.
　　ISBN 978-1-4143-4555-0 (hc)
　　1. Heaven—Christianity—Meditations. I. Title.
　　BT846.3.A4335 2012
　　236'.24—dc23　　　　　　　　　　　　　　　　　　　　　　2011033853

Printed in China

18　17　16　15　14　13　12
7　6　5　4　3　2　1

CONTENTS

Eternal Promises

The LORD will fulfill his purpose for me;
    your love, O LORD, endures forever.

PSALM 138:8

"I know the plans I have for you," declares the LORD,
"plans to prosper you and not to harm you, plans to
give you hope and a future."

JEREMIAH 29:11

Our Desire Is God's Idea

Charles Spurgeon expressed this perspective on death: "To come to Thee is to come home from exile, to come to land out of the raging storm, to come to rest after long labour, to come to the goal of my desires and the summit of my wishes."[1]

What God made us to desire, and therefore what we *do* desire if we admit it, is exactly what he promises to those who follow Jesus Christ: a resurrected life in a resurrected body, with the resurrected Christ on a resurrected Earth. Our desires correspond precisely to God's plans. It's not that we want something, so we engage in wishful thinking that what we want exists. It's the opposite—the reason we want it is precisely because God has planned for it to exist. Resurrected people living in a resurrected universe isn't our idea—it's *God's*.

Eternal Promises

The LORD God formed the man from the dust of the ground and breathed into his nostrils the breath of life, and the man became a living being.

GENESIS 2:7

The Spirit of God has made me;
the breath of the Almighty gives me life.

JOB 33:4

Let Your Heavenly Imagination Soar

As human beings, whom God made to be both physical and spiritual, we are not designed to live in a non-physical realm—indeed, we are incapable of even imagining such a place (or, rather, *non*-place). An incorporeal state is not only unfamiliar to our experience, it is also incompatible with our God-given constitution. We are not, as Plato supposed, merely spiritual beings temporarily encased in bodies.

Adam did not become a "living being"—the Hebrew word *nephesh*—until he was both body *and* spirit (Genesis 2:7). We are physical beings as much as we are spiritual beings. That's why our bodily resurrection is essential to endow us with eternal righteous humanity, setting us free from sin, the Curse, and death.

We cannot anticipate or desire what we cannot imagine. That's why, I believe, God has given us glimpses of Heaven in the Bible—to fire up our imaginations and kindle a desire for Heaven in our hearts.

Eternal Promises

The LORD God had planted a garden in the east, in Eden; and there he put the man he had formed. And the LORD God made all kinds of trees grow out of the ground—trees that were pleasing to the eye and good for food.

GENESIS 2:8-9

God, the LORD, created the heavens and stretched
        them out.
    He created the earth and everything in it.
He gives breath to everyone,
    life to everyone who walks the earth.

ISAIAH 42:5, NLT

Hinting at What's to Come

Scripture provides us with a substantial amount of information, direct and indirect, about the world to come, with enough detail to help us envision it, but not so much as to make us think we can completely wrap our minds around it. I believe that God expects us to use our imagination, even as we recognize its limitations and flaws. If God didn't want us to imagine what Heaven will be like, he wouldn't have told us as much about it as he has.

In order to get a picture of Heaven—which will one day be centered on the New Earth—you don't need to look up at the clouds; you simply need to look around you and imagine what all this would be like without sin and death and suffering and corruption.

Eternal Promises

When I consider your heavens,
    the work of your fingers,
the moon and the stars,
    which you have set in place,
what is man that you are mindful of him,
    the son of man that you care for him?

PSALM 8:3-4

How many are your works, O LORD!
    In wisdom you made them all;
    the earth is full of your creatures.

PSALM 104:24

Get Ready to Marvel

When I anticipate my first glimpse of Heaven,
I remember the first time I went snorkeling. I saw
countless fish of every shape, size, and color. And just
when I thought I'd seen the most beautiful fish, along
came another even more striking. Etched in my memory is a certain sound—the sound of a gasp going
through my rubber snorkel as my eyes were opened
to that breathtaking underwater world.

I imagine our first glimpse of Heaven will cause
us to similarly gasp in amazement and delight. That
initial gasp will likely be followed by many more as
we continually encounter new sights in that endlessly
wonderful place. And that will be just the beginning,
because we'll not see our real eternal home—the New
Earth—until after the resurrection of the dead. And
though we can imagine wonderful things, our new
home will be better by far.

Eternal Promises

Let them praise the name of the LORD,
    for he commanded and they were created.
He set them in place for ever and ever;
    he gave a decree that will never pass away. . . .
Let them praise the name of the LORD,
    for his name alone is exalted;
        his splendor is above the earth and the heavens.

PSALM 148:5-6, 13

Blessed is the man [whose] . . . delight is in the law of
        the LORD,
    and on his law he meditates day and night.
He is like a tree planted by streams of water,
    which yields its fruit in season
and whose leaf does not wither.
    Whatever he does prospers.

PSALM 1:1-3

Look Around, Then Envision More

Look out a window. Take a walk. Talk with your friend. Use your God-given skills to paint or draw or build a shed or write a book. But imagine Earth—all of it—in its original condition. The happy dog with the wagging tail. The flowers unwilted, the grass undying, the blue sky without pollution. People smiling and joyful. If you're not in a particularly beautiful place, close your eyes and envision the most beautiful place you've ever been—complete with palm trees, raging rivers, jagged mountains, waterfalls, or snowdrifts.

Think of friends or family members who loved Jesus and are with him now. Picture them with you, walking together. All of you have powerful bodies, stronger than those of an Olympic decathlete. You are laughing, playing, talking, and reminiscing. You reach up into a tree to pick an apple or orange. You take a bite. It's so sweet that it's startling. You've never tasted anything so good. That's Heaven—on Earth. And it's the blood-bought promise of God!

Eternal Promises

My soul yearns, even faints,
    for the courts of the LORD;
my heart and my flesh cry out
    for the living God.

PSALM 84:2

The God of all grace, who called you to his eternal
glory in Christ, after you have suffered a little while,
will himself restore you and make you strong, firm
and steadfast.

1 PETER 5:10

Jesus Awaits Your Arrival

You see someone coming toward you. It's Jesus, with a big smile on his face. You fall to your knees in worship. He pulls you up and embraces you. At last, you're with the person you were made for, in the place you were made to be.

"Set your hearts on things above, where Christ is seated at the right hand of God" (Colossians 3:1). This is a direct command to set our hearts on Heaven. And to make sure we don't miss the importance of a heaven-centered life, the next verse says, "Set your minds on things above, not on earthly things." God commands us to set our hearts and minds on Heaven.

To long for Christ is to long for Heaven, for that is where we'll be with him. God's people are "longing for a better country" (Hebrews 11:16). We cannot set our eyes on Christ without setting our eyes on Heaven, and we cannot set our eyes on Heaven without setting our eyes on Christ.

Eternal Promises

The end of all things is near. Therefore be clear minded and self-controlled so that you can pray.

1 PETER 4:7

Since we are surrounded by such a great cloud of witnesses, . . . let us run with perseverance the race marked out for us. Let us fix our eyes on Jesus, the author and perfecter of our faith, who for the joy set before him endured the cross, scorning its shame, and sat down at the right hand of the throne of God.

HEBREWS 12:1-2

In Pursuit of Heaven

"Set your hearts on things above, where Christ is seated at the right hand of God" (Colossians 3:1).

The Greek word translated "set your hearts on" is *zeteo*, which "denotes man's general philosophical search or quest."[2] It is a diligent, active, single-minded investigation. So we can understand Paul's admonition in Colossians 3:1 as follows: "Diligently, actively, single-mindedly pursue the things above"—in a word, *Heaven*.

The verb *zeteo* is in the present tense, suggesting an ongoing process. "Keep seeking heaven." Don't just have a conversation, read a book, or listen to a sermon and feel as if you've fulfilled the command. Since you'll spend the next lifetime living in Heaven, why not spend this lifetime seeking Heaven—eagerly anticipating and preparing for it?

Our minds are so much set on Earth that we are unaccustomed to heavenly thinking. So we must work at it. What have you been doing daily to set your mind on things above, to *seek* Heaven?

Eternal Promises

Thanks be to God! He gives us the victory through our
Lord Jesus Christ.

1 CORINTHIANS 15:57

Praise be to the Lord, the God of Israel,
    because he has come and has redeemed his people.
He has raised up a horn of salvation for us
    in the house of his servant David.

LUKE 1:68-69

The Road to Heaven

If we understood Hell even the slightest bit, none of us would ever say, "Go to Hell." It is far too easy to go to Hell. It requires no change of course, no navigational adjustments. We were born with our autopilot set toward Hell. It is nothing to take lightly—Hell is the single greatest tragedy in the universe.

God loves us enough to tell us the truth—there are two eternal destinations, not one, and we must choose the right path if we are to go to Heaven. All roads do not lead to Heaven. Only one does: Jesus Christ. He said, "No one comes to the Father except through me" (John 14:6). All other roads lead to Hell. The high stakes involved in the choice between Heaven and Hell will cause us to appreciate Heaven in deeper ways, never taking it for granted, and always praising God for his grace that delivers us from what we deserve and grants us forever what we don't.

Eternal Promises

If serving the LORD seems undesirable to you, then choose for yourselves this day whom you will serve, whether the gods your forefathers served beyond the River, or the gods of the Amorites, in whose land you are living. But as for me and my household, we will serve the LORD.

JOSHUA 24:15

The wages of sin is death, but the gift of God is eternal life in Christ Jesus our Lord.

ROMANS 6:23

The Best Gift Ever

The best of life on Earth is a glimpse of Heaven; the worst of life is a glimpse of Hell. For Christians, this present life is the closest they will come to Hell. For unbelievers, it is the closest they will come to Heaven.

Jesus asks a haunting question in Mark 8:36-37: "What good is it for a man to gain the whole world, yet forfeit his soul? Or what can a man give in exchange for his soul?"

The price has been paid. But still, we must choose. Like any gift, forgiveness can be offered, but it isn't ours until we choose to receive it. A convicted criminal can be offered a pardon by the governor, but if he or she rejects the pardon, it's not valid. A pardon must be accepted. Similarly, Christ offers each of us the gift of forgiveness and eternal life—but just because the offer is made doesn't make it ours. To have it, we must choose to accept it.

Eternal Promises

God presented [Jesus] as a sacrifice of atonement, through faith in his blood.

ROMANS 3:25

This is the testimony: God has given us eternal life, and this life is in his Son. He who has the Son has life; he who does not have the Son of God does not have life.

I JOHN 5:11-12

It's a Package Deal

Can we really know in advance where we're going when we die? The apostle John, the same one who wrote about the new heavens and New Earth, said in one of his letters, "I write these things to you who believe in the name of the Son of God so that *you may know that you have eternal life*" (1 John 5:13, emphasis added). We *can* know for sure that we have eternal life. We *can* know for sure that we will go to Heaven when we die.

"Seek the LORD while he may be found; call on him while he is near" (Isaiah 55:6).

Have you confessed your sins? asked Christ to forgive you? placed your trust in Christ's death and resurrection on your behalf? asked Jesus to be your Lord and empower you to follow him? You are made for a person and a place. Jesus is the person. Heaven is the place. They are a package—you cannot get Heaven without Jesus or Jesus without Heaven. We will explore Heaven's joys and wonders throughout this book. But we dare not presume we can enter Heaven apart from Christ.

Eternal Promises

Your dead will live;
  their bodies will rise.
You who dwell in the dust,
  wake up and shout for joy.

ISAIAH 26:19

The Lord himself will come down from heaven, with a loud command, with the voice of the archangel and with the trumpet call of God, and the dead in Christ will rise first. After that, we who are still alive and are left will be caught up together with them in the clouds to meet the Lord in the air. And so we will be with the Lord forever.

1 THESSALONIANS 4:16-17

What Happens When You Die?

The answer to the question "Will we live in Heaven forever?" depends on what we mean by Heaven. Will we be with the Lord forever? Absolutely. Will we always be with him in exactly the same place that Heaven is now? No. In the present Heaven, we'll be in Christ's presence, and we'll be joyful, but we'll be looking forward to our bodily resurrection and permanent relocation to the New Earth.

It bears repeating because it is so commonly misunderstood: *When we die, believers in Christ will not go to the Heaven where we'll live forever.* Instead, we'll go to an intermediate Heaven. In that Heaven—where those who died covered by Christ's blood are now—we'll await the time of Christ's return to the earth, our bodily resurrection, the final judgment, and the creation of the new heavens and New Earth.

Eternal Promises

Lord, you have been our dwelling place
     throughout all generations.
Before the mountains were born
     or you brought forth the earth and the world,
     from everlasting to everlasting you are God.

PSALM 90:1-2

To the only God our Savior be glory, majesty, power
and authority, through Jesus Christ our Lord, before
all ages, now and forevermore!

JUDE 1:25

From Temporary to Permanent

Only God is eternal and self-existent. All else is created. Heaven is not synonymous with God, nor is it part of his essential being. Therefore, God must have created Heaven. It is not a place where he *must* dwell, but it is where he *chooses* to dwell.

Because God created Heaven, it had a beginning and is therefore neither timeless nor changeless. It had a past (the time prior to Christ's incarnation, death, and resurrection), it has a present (the Heaven where believers go when they die), and it will have a future (the eternal Heaven, or New Earth). The past Heaven, the present Heaven, and the future or eternal Heaven can all be called Heaven, yet *they are not synonymous*, even though they are all God's dwelling places.

The present Heaven is a temporary lodging, a waiting place until the return of Christ and our bodily resurrection. The eternal Heaven, the New Earth, is our true home, the place where we will live forever with our Lord and each other.

Eternal Promises

I will put my dwelling place among you, and I will not abhor you. I will walk among you and be your God, and you will be my people.

LEVITICUS 26:11-12

[Jesus said.] "If I go and prepare a place for you, I will come back and take you to be with me that you also may be where I am."

JOHN 14:3

At Home with God

That God would come down to the New Earth to live with us fits perfectly with his original plan. God could have taken Adam and Eve up to Heaven to visit with him in his world. Instead, he came down to walk with them in their world (Genesis 3:8). Jesus says of anyone who would be his disciple, "My Father will love him, and we will come to him and make our home with him" (John 14:23). This is a picture that fits perfectly with God's original, ultimate plan—not to take us up to live in a realm made for him, but to come down and live with us *in the realm he made for us.*

Eternal Promises

Stephen, full of the Holy Spirit, looked up to heaven
and saw the glory of God, and Jesus standing at the
right hand of God. "Look," he said, "I see heaven
open and the Son of Man standing at the right hand
of God."

ACTS 7:55-56

In the year that King Uzziah died, I saw the Lord
seated on a throne, high and exalted, and the train
of his robe filled the temple.

ISAIAH 6:1

A Dimension Seldom Seen

The present Heaven is normally invisible to those living on Earth. For those who have trouble accepting the reality of an unseen realm, consider the perspective of cutting-edge researchers who embrace string theory. Scientists at Yale, Princeton, and Stanford, among others, postulate that there are ten unobservable dimensions and likely an infinite number of imperceptible universes.[3] If this is what leading scientists believe, why should anyone feel self-conscious about believing in *one* unobservable dimension, a realm containing angels and Heaven and Hell?

The Bible teaches that sometimes humans are allowed to see into Heaven. When Stephen was being stoned because of his faith in Christ, he gazed into Heaven. Scripture tells us not that Stephen dreamed this, but that he actually *saw* it. It seems likely that God didn't merely create a vision for Stephen in order to make Heaven *appear* physical. Rather, he allowed Stephen to see an intermediate Heaven that *was* (and *is*) physical.

Eternal Promises

How lovely is your dwelling place, O LORD Almighty!

PSALM 84:1

[Jesus said,] "To him who overcomes, I will give the right to eat from the tree of life, which is in the paradise of God."

REVELATION 2:7

A Garden Paradise

During the Crucifixion, when Jesus said to the thief on the cross, "Today you will be with me in paradise" (Luke 23:43), he was referring to the present Heaven. But why did he call it *paradise*, and what did he mean? The word *paradise* comes from the Persian word *pairi-daeza*, meaning "a walled park" or "enclosed garden." It was used to describe the great walled gardens of the Persian king Cyrus's royal palaces. In the Septuagint, the Greek translation of the Old Testament, the Greek word for paradise is used to describe the Garden of Eden (e.g., Genesis 2:8; Ezekiel 28:13). Later, because of the Jewish belief that God would restore Eden, *paradise* became the word to describe the eternal state of the righteous, and to a lesser extent, the present Heaven.[4]

The word *paradise* does not refer to wild nature but to nature under mankind's dominion. The garden or park was not left to grow entirely on its own. People brought their creativity to bear on managing, cultivating, and presenting the garden or park.

Eternal Promises

After [God] drove the man out, he placed on the east side of the Garden of Eden cherubim and a flaming sword flashing back and forth to guard the way to the tree of life.

GENESIS 3:24

No longer will there be any curse. The throne of God and of the Lamb will be in the city, and his servants will serve him.

REVELATION 22:3

Eden as It Was Meant to Be

After the Fall, it appears that Eden's Paradise, with the tree of life, retained its identity as a physical place but was no longer accessible to mankind. It was guarded by cherubim, who are residents of Heaven, where God is "enthroned between the cherubim" (2 Kings 19:15). Eden was not destroyed. What was destroyed was mankind's ability to live in Eden. There's no indication that Eden was stripped of its physicality and transformed into a "spiritual" entity. It appears to have remained just as it was, a physical paradise removed to a realm we can't gain access to—most likely the present Heaven, because we know for certain that's where the tree of life now is (Revelation 2:7).

God is not done with Eden. He preserved it not as a museum piece but as a place that mankind will one day occupy again.

Eternal Promises

From heaven the LORD looks down
    and sees all mankind;
from his dwelling place he watches
    all who live on earth.

PSALM 33:13-14

Those who feared the LORD talked with each
other, and the LORD listened and heard. A scroll of
remembrance was written in his presence concerning
those who feared the LORD and honored his name.

MALACHI 3:16

Remembering Earth as It Was, in Heaven

God keeps a record in Heaven of what *everyone* does on Earth. We know that record will outlast our life on Earth—for believers, at least until the judgment seat of Christ (2 Corinthians 5:10); for unbelievers, right up until the Great White Throne Judgment (Revelation 20:11-13), just preceding the coming of the new heavens and New Earth. For those now in Heaven, records of life on Earth still exist.

Memory is a basic element of personality. If we are truly *ourselves* in Heaven, there must be continuity of memory from Earth to Heaven. We will not be different people, but the same people marvelously relocated and transformed. Heaven cleanses us but does not revise or extinguish our origins or history. Undoubtedly we will remember God's works of grace in our lives that comforted, assured, sustained, and empowered us to live for him.

Eternal Promises

Maidens will dance and be glad,
    young men and old as well.
I will turn their mourning into gladness;
    I will give them comfort and joy instead of sorrow.

JEREMIAH 31:13

We are surrounded by such a great cloud of witnesses.

HEBREWS 12:1

A Cause for Celebration

Christ said, "There will be more rejoicing in heaven over one sinner who repents than over ninety-nine righteous persons who do not need to repent" (Luke 15:7). Similarly, "there is rejoicing in the presence of the angels of God over one sinner who repents" (Luke 15:10). Notice it does not speak of rejoicing *by* the angels but *in the presence* of angels. Who is doing this rejoicing in Heaven? I believe it logically includes not only God but also the saints in Heaven, who would so deeply appreciate the wonder of human conversion—especially the conversion of those they knew and loved on Earth. If they rejoice over conversions happening on Earth, then obviously *they must be aware of what is happening on Earth*—and not just generally, but specifically, down to the details of individuals coming to faith in Christ.

Eternal Promises

[Jesus] is able to save completely those who come to God through him, because he always lives to intercede for them.

HEBREWS 7:25

I saw under the altar the souls of those who had been slain because of the word of God and the testimony they had maintained. They called out in a loud voice, "How long, Sovereign Lord, holy and true, until you judge the inhabitants of the earth and avenge our blood?"

REVELATION 6:9-10

Prayers Coming Down from Heaven

Christ, the God-man, is in Heaven, at the right hand of God, interceding for people on Earth (Romans 8:34). This means at least one person who has died has gone to Heaven and is now praying for those on Earth. The martyrs in Heaven also pray to God (Revelation 6:10), asking him to take specific action on Earth. They are praying for God's justice, which has intercessory implications for Christians now suffering here. The sense of connection and loyalty to the body of Christ—and concern for the saints on Earth—would likely be enhanced, not diminished, by being in Heaven (Ephesians 3:15). In any case, Revelation 6:9-11 shows us that some who have died and are now in Heaven are praying concerning what's happening on Earth.

Eternal Promises

There will be more rejoicing in heaven over one sinner who repents than over ninety-nine righteous persons who do not need to repent.

LUKE 15:7

The prayer of a righteous man is powerful and effective.

JAMES 5:16

Watching from Above

If prayer is simply talking to God, presumably we will pray more in Heaven than we do now—not less. And given our righteous state in Heaven, our prayers will be more effective than ever (James 5:16). Revelation 5:8 speaks of the "prayers of the saints" in a context that may include saints in Heaven, not just on Earth. We are never told to pray *to* the saints, but only to God. Yet the saints may well be praying for us.

People in Heaven are not frail beings whose joy can only be preserved by shielding them from what's really going on in the universe. Happiness in Heaven is not based on ignorance but on perspective. Those who live in the presence of Christ find great joy in worshiping God and living as righteous beings in rich fellowship in a sinless environment. And because God is continuously at work on Earth, the saints watching from Heaven have a great deal to praise him for, including God's drawing people on Earth to himself (Luke 15:7, 10).

Eternal Promises

Blessed are those who dwell in your house;
    they are ever praising you.

PSALM 84:4

Praise the LORD.
I will extol the LORD with all my heart
    in the council of the upright and in the assembly.
Great are the works of the LORD;
    they are pondered by all who delight in them.

PSALM 111:1-2

Where Loved Ones Are Waiting

Those in the present Heaven are looking forward to Christ's return, their bodily resurrection, the final judgment, and the fashioning of the New Earth from the ruins of the old. Only then and there, in our eternal home, will all evil and suffering and sorrow be washed away by the hand of God. Only then and there will we experience the fullness of joy intended by God and purchased for us by Christ at an unfathomable cost.

Meanwhile, we on this dying Earth can relax and rejoice for our loved ones who are in the presence of Christ. As the apostle Paul tells us, though we naturally grieve at losing loved ones, we are not "to grieve like the rest of men, who have no hope" (1 Thessalonians 4:13). Our parting is not the end of our relationship, only an interruption. We have not "lost" them, because we know where they are. They are experiencing the joy of Christ's presence in a place so wonderful that Christ called it Paradise. And we're told that one day, in a magnificent reunion, they and we "will be with the Lord forever. Therefore encourage each other with these words" (1 Thessalonians 4:17-18).

Eternal Promises

The earth is the LORD's, and everything in it,
  the world, and all who live in it.

PSALM 24:1

He carried me away in the Spirit to a mountain great
and high, and showed me the Holy City, Jerusalem,
coming down out of heaven from God.

REVELATION 21:10

A Place Just for Us

We long for a return to Paradise—a perfect world, without the corruption of sin, where God walks with us and talks with us in the cool of the day. Because we're human beings, we desire something tangible and physical, something that will not fade away. And that is exactly what God promises us—a home that will not be destroyed, a kingdom that will not fade, a city with unshakable foundations, an incorruptible inheritance.

Adam was formed from the dust of the earth, forever establishing our connection to the earth (Genesis 2:7). Just as we are made *from* the earth, so too we are made *for* the earth. But, you may object, Jesus said he was going to prepare a place for us where we will live with him forever (John 14:2-3). Yes. But *what is that place?* the New Earth (Revelation 21). That's where the New Jerusalem will reside when it comes down out of Heaven. Only *then* will we be truly home.

Eternal Promises

In keeping with [God's] promise we are looking forward to a new heaven and a new earth, the home of righteousness.

2 PETER 3:13

The angel showed me the river of the water of life, as clear as crystal, flowing from the throne of God and of the Lamb.

REVELATION 22:1

Feeling Right at Home

Scripture gives us images full of hints and implications about Heaven. Put them together, and these jigsaw pieces form a beautiful picture. For example, we're told that Heaven is a city (Hebrews 11:10; 13:14). When we hear the word *city*, we shouldn't scratch our heads and think, "I wonder what that means?" We understand cities. Cities have buildings, culture, art, music, athletics, goods and services, events of all kinds. And, of course, cities have *people* engaged in activities, gatherings, conversations, and work.

Heaven is also described as a country (Hebrews 11:16). We know about countries. They have territories, rulers, national interests, pride in their identity, and citizens who are both diverse and unified.

If we can't imagine our present Earth without rivers, mountains, trees, and flowers, then why would we try to imagine the New Earth without these features? We wouldn't expect a non-Earth to have mountains and rivers. But God doesn't promise us a non-Earth. He promises us a *New* Earth. If the word *Earth* in this phrase means anything, it means that we can expect to find earthly things there—including atmosphere, mountains, water, trees, people, houses—even cities, buildings, and streets. (These familiar features are specifically mentioned in Revelation 21–22.)

Eternal Promises

The LORD your God is with you,
    he is mighty to save.
He will take great delight in you,
    he will quiet you with his love,
        he will rejoice over you with singing.

ZEPHANIAH 3:17

God was pleased to have all his fullness dwell
in [Christ].

COLOSSIANS 1:19

Making the Invisible Physical

The present Earth is as much a valid reference point for envisioning the New Earth as our present bodies are a valid reference point for envisioning our new bodies. After all, we're living on the remnants of a perfect world, as the remnants of a perfect humanity. We shouldn't read into the New Earth anything that's wrong with this one, but can we not imagine what it would be like to be unhindered by disease and death? Can we not envision natural beauty untainted by destruction?

The idea of the New Earth as a physical place isn't an invention of shortsighted human imagination. Rather, it's the invention of a transcendent God, who made physical human beings to live on a physical Earth, *and* who chose to become a man himself on that same Earth. He did this that he might redeem mankind *and* Earth. Why? In order to glorify himself and enjoy forever the company of men and women in a world he's made for us.

Eternal Promises

In your unfailing love you will lead
    the people you have redeemed.
In your strength you will guide them
    to your holy dwelling.

EXODUS 15:13

[God] has reconciled you by Christ's physical body
through death to present you holy in his sight, without
blemish and free from accusation.

COLOSSIANS 1:22

God's Love Language

God has never given up on his original creation. An entire biblical vocabulary makes this point obvious. *Reconcile. Redeem. Restore. Recover. Return. Renew. Regenerate. Resurrect.* Each of these biblical words begins with the *re-* prefix, suggesting a return to an original condition that was ruined or lost. For example, *redemption* means to buy back what was formerly owned. Similarly, *reconciliation* means the restoration or reestablishment of a prior friendship or unity. *Renewal* means to make new again, restoring to an original state. *Resurrection* means becoming physically alive again, after death.

These words emphasize that God always sees us in light of what he intended us to be, and he always seeks to *restore* us to that design. Likewise, he sees the earth in terms of what he intended it to be, and he seeks to restore it to its original design.

Eternal Promises

When the kindness and love of God our Savior
appeared, he saved us, not because of righteous things
we had done, but because of his mercy. He saved us
through the washing of rebirth and renewal by the
Holy Spirit, whom he poured out on us generously
through Jesus Christ our Savior, so that, having been
justified by his grace, we might become heirs having
the hope of eternal life.

TITUS 3:4-7

It was not with perishable things such as silver or gold
that you were redeemed . . . but with the precious
blood of Christ, a lamb without blemish or defect.

1 PETER 1:18-19

Jesus, Our Redeemer

Luke tells the story of the prophetess Anna, a woman in her eighties, who worshiped at the Temple night and day, fasting and praying (Luke 2:36-38). Upon seeing the baby Jesus, she "gave thanks to God and spoke about the child to all who were looking forward to the redemption of Jerusalem" (v. 38).

Notice Luke's exact wording. What were God's people looking forward to? *Redemption.* Their own redemption? Of course. But it was much more than that. It was the redemption of their families and community and even their city, Jerusalem. The redemption of Jerusalem would also be the redemption of Israel. As the entire world was promised blessing through Abraham, the redemption of Jerusalem and Israel speaks of the redemption of the earth itself.

And who would be the agent of that redemption? Jesus, this child, the Messiah who would become King not only of redeemed individuals, but also King of a redeemed Jerusalem, and King of a redeemed earth. This is the gospel of the Kingdom.

Eternal Promises

As in Adam all die, so in Christ all will be made alive.
But each in his own turn: Christ, the firstfruits; then,
when he comes, those who belong to him. Then the
end will come, when he hands over the kingdom to
God the Father after he has destroyed all dominion,
authority and power. For he must reign until he has
put all his enemies under his feet.

1 CORINTHIANS 15:22-25

Our citizenship is in heaven. And we eagerly await a
Savior from there, the Lord Jesus Christ, who, by the
power that enables him to bring everything under his
control, will transform our lowly bodies so that they
will be like his glorious body.

PHILIPPIANS 3:20-21

Christ's Mission, Our Mission

Our present purpose is inseparable from God's stated eternal purpose for us to rule the earth forever as his children and heirs. That is at the core of the Westminster Shorter Catechism's defining statement: "Man's chief end is to glorify God, and to enjoy him forever."[5] We will glorify God and find joy in him as we do what he has made us to do: serve him as resurrected beings and carry out his plan for developing a Christ-centered, resurrected culture in a resurrected universe.

Christ's mission is both to redeem what was lost in the Fall and to destroy all competitors to God's dominion, authority, and power. When everything is put under his feet, when God rules all and mankind rules the earth as kings under Christ, the King of kings, all will finally be as God intends. The period of rebellion will be over forever, and the universe, and all who serve Christ, will participate in the Master's joy!

Eternal Promises

Praise be to his glorious name forever;
    may the whole earth be filled with his glory.
                                    Amen and Amen.

PSALM 72:19

The earth will be filled with the knowledge of the
        glory of the LORD,
    as the waters cover the sea.

HABAKKUK 2:14

Our Future World Secured

God's Kingdom and dominion are not about what happens in some remote, unearthly place; instead, they are about what happens on Earth, which God created for his glory. God has tied his glory to the earth and everything connected with it: mankind, animals, trees, rivers, *everything*. "Holy, holy, holy is the LORD Almighty; the whole earth is full of his glory" (Isaiah 6:3). The Hebrew here can be translated "the fullness of the earth is his glory." His glory is manifested in his creation. The earth is not disposable. It is essential to God's plan. God promises that ultimately the whole Earth will be filled with his glory (Psalm 72:19; Habakkuk 2:14).

God has his hands on the earth. He will not let go—even when it requires that his hands be pierced by nails. Both his incarnation and those nails secured him to Earth and its eternal future. In a redemptive work far larger than most imagine, Christ bought and paid for our future and the earth's.

Eternal Promises

Let the heavens rejoice, let the earth be glad;
>   let them say among the nations, "The LORD
>   reigns!"
Let the sea resound, and all that is in it;
>   let the fields be jubilant, and everything in them!

1 CHRONICLES 16:31-32

Every good and perfect gift is from above, coming
down from the Father of the heavenly lights, who does
not change like shifting shadows. He chose to give us
birth through the word of truth, that we might be a
kind of firstfruits of all he created.

JAMES 1:17-18

Earth and Heaven Will Be One

God's plan of the ages is "to bring all things in heaven and on earth together under one head, even Christ" (Ephesians 1:10). "All things" is broad and inclusive—nothing will be left out. This verse corresponds precisely to the culmination of history that we see enacted in Revelation 21, the merging together of the once separate realms of Heaven and Earth, fully under Christ's lordship.

The hymn "This Is My Father's World" expresses this truth in its final words: "Jesus who died shall be satisfied, and earth and heaven be one."[6] Just as God and mankind are reconciled in Christ, so too the dwellings of God and mankind—Heaven and Earth—will be reconciled in Christ. As God and man will be forever united in Jesus, so Heaven and Earth will forever be united in the new physical universe where we will live as resurrected beings.

Eternal Promises

[God] made known to us the mystery of his will . . .
to be put into effect when the times will have reached
their fulfillment—to bring all things in heaven and on
earth together under one head, even Christ.

EPHESIANS 1:9-10

We wait for the blessed hope—the glorious appearing
of our great God and Savior, Jesus Christ, who gave
himself for us to redeem us from all wickedness and to
purify for himself a people that are his very own, eager
to do what is good.

TITUS 2:13-14

No More Gulf between Heaven and Earth

Heaven is God's home. Earth is our home. Jesus Christ, as the God-man, forever links God and mankind, and thereby forever links Heaven and Earth. As Ephesians 1:10 demonstrates, this idea of Earth and Heaven becoming one is explicitly biblical. Christ will make Earth into Heaven and Heaven into Earth. Just as the wall that separates God and mankind is torn down in Jesus, so too the wall that separates Heaven and Earth will be forever demolished. "Now the dwelling of God is with men, and he will live with them" (Revelation 21:3). God will live with us on the New Earth.

God's plan is that there will be no more gulf between the spiritual and physical worlds. There will be no divided loyalties or divided realms. There will be one cosmos, one universe united under one Lord—forever. This is the unstoppable plan of God. This is where history is headed.

Eternal Promises

When all things are under his authority, the Son will
put himself under God's authority, so that God, who
gave his Son authority over all things, will be utterly
supreme over everything everywhere.

1 CORINTHIANS 15:28, NLT

I, Jesus, have sent my angel to give you this message
for the churches. I am both the source of David and
the heir to his throne. I am the bright morning star.

REVELATION 22:16, NLT

Reigning beside Jesus

The Bible's central storyline revolves around a question: Who will reign over the earth? Earth's destiny hangs in the balance. Because it is the realm where God's glory has been most challenged and resisted, it is therefore also the stage on which his glory will be most graphically demonstrated. By reclaiming, restoring, renewing, and resurrecting Earth—and empowering a regenerated mankind to reign over it— God will accomplish his purpose of bringing glory to himself.

Ultimately, Satan will be eternally dethroned and God will be permanently enthroned. Christ will become the unchallenged, absolute ruler of the universe and then will turn over to his Father the Kingdom he has won (1 Corinthians 15:28). Redeemed humans will be God's unchallenged, delegated rulers of the New Earth. God and humanity will live together in eternal happiness, forever deepening their relationships, as the glory of God permeates every aspect of the new creation.

Eternal Promises

Having disarmed the powers and authorities, [Christ] made a public spectacle of them, triumphing over them by the cross.

COLOSSIANS 2:15

[Jesus said,] "On this rock I will build my church, and the gates of Hades will not overcome it."

MATTHEW 16:18

Victory with Jesus

Christ came not to destroy the world he created, but to destroy the works of the devil, which were to twist and pervert and ruin what God had made. Christ's redemptive work will forever destroy the devil's work by removing its hold on creation, and reversing its consequences. It is Satan's desire to destroy the world. God's intent is not to destroy the world but to deliver it from destruction. His plan is to redeem this fallen world, which he designed for greatness.

Redeemed mankind will reign with Christ over the earth. The gates of Satan's false kingdom will not prevail against Christ's church (Matthew 16:18).

The outcome of the great war is not in question. It is certain. Christ will reign victoriously forever. The only question we must answer is this: Will we fight on his side or against him? We answer this question not just once, with our words, but daily, with our choices.

Eternal Promises

After my skin has been destroyed,
    yet in my flesh I will see God;
I myself will see him
    with my own eyes—I, and not another.
    How my heart yearns within me!

JOB 19:26-27

The body is . . . for the Lord, and the Lord for the
body. And God both raised up the Lord and will
also raise us up by His power.

1 CORINTHIANS 6:13-14, NKJV

The Same, Only Different

"If anyone is in Christ, he is a new creation; the old has gone, the new has come!" (2 Corinthians 5:17). Becoming a new creation sounds as if it involves a radical change, and indeed it does. But though we become *new* people when we come to Christ, we still remain the *same* people.

When I came to Christ as a high school student, I became a new person, yet I was still the same person I'd always been. My mother saw a lot of changes, but she still recognized me. My dog never once growled at me—he knew who I was. I was still Randy Alcorn, though a substantially transformed Randy Alcorn. This same me will undergo another change at death, and yet another change at the resurrection of the dead. But through all the changes *I will still be who I was and who I am.* There will be continuity from this life to the next.

Eternal Promises

After his suffering, [Jesus] showed himself to these men and gave many convincing proofs that he was alive. He appeared to them over a period of forty days and spoke about the kingdom of God.

ACTS 1:3

Dear friends, now we are children of God, and what we will be has not yet been made known. But we know that when he appears, we shall be like him, for we shall see him as he is.

1 JOHN 3:2

We Shall Be like Him

We have an example in Scripture of what a resurrection body is like. We're told a great deal about Christ's resurrected body, and we're told that our bodies will be like his. The empty tomb is the ultimate proof that Christ's resurrection body was the same body that died on the cross. If *resurrection* meant the creation of a new body, Christ's original body would have remained in the tomb.

When Jesus said to his disciples after his resurrection, "It is I myself," he was emphasizing to them that he was the same person—in spirit *and* body—who had gone to the cross (Luke 24:39). His disciples saw the marks of his crucifixion, unmistakable evidence that this was the same body.

Jesus walked the earth in his resurrection body for forty days, showing us how we would live as resurrected human beings. In effect, he also demonstrated *where* we would live as resurrected human beings—on Earth. Christ's resurrection body was suited for life on Earth, not primarily life in the intermediate Heaven. As Jesus was raised to come back to live on Earth, so we will be raised to come back to live on Earth (1 Thessalonians 4:14; Revelation 21:1-3).

Eternal Promises

The two told what had happened . . . and how Jesus was recognized by them when he broke the bread. While they were still talking about this, Jesus himself stood among them. . . . He said to them, "Why are you troubled . . . ? Look at my hands and my feet. It is I myself!"

LUKE 24:35-36, 38-39

Jesus came and stood among them and said, "Peace be with you!" Then he said to Thomas, "Put your finger here; see my hands. Reach out your hand and put it into my side. Stop doubting and believe."

JOHN 20:26-27

Resurrected, but Remarkably Familiar

The times Jesus spent with his disciples after his resurrection were remarkably normal. Early one morning, he "stood on the shore" at a distance (John 21:4). He didn't hover or float—or even walk on water, though he could have. He stood, then called to the disciples (v. 5). Obviously his voice sounded human, because it traveled across the water and the disciples didn't suspect it was anyone but a human. It apparently didn't sound like the deep, otherworldly voices that movies assign to God or angels.

Jesus had started a fire, and he was already cooking fish that he'd presumably caught himself. He cooked them, which means he didn't just snap his fingers and materialize a finished meal. He invited the disciples to add their fish to his and said, "Come and have breakfast" (John 21:12).

Once we understand that Christ's resurrection is the prototype for the resurrection of mankind and the earth, we realize that Scripture has given us an interpretive precedent for approaching passages concerning human resurrection and life on the New Earth.

Eternal Promises

You, O God, are my king from of old;
    you bring salvation upon the earth. . . .
The day is yours, and yours also the night;
    you established the sun and moon.
It was you who set all the boundaries of the earth;
    you made both summer and winter.

PSALM 74:12, 16-17

I know that the LORD is great,
    that our Lord is greater than all gods.
The LORD does whatever pleases him,
    in the heavens and on the earth,
    in the seas and all their depths.
He makes clouds rise from the ends of the earth;
    he sends lightning with the rain
    and brings out the wind from his storehouses.

PSALM 135:5-7

A Magnificent Universe

Eugene Peterson captures the universal implications of Christ's redemption when he paraphrases Colossians 1:18-20 in *The Message*: "He was supreme in the beginning and—leading the resurrection parade—he is supreme in the end. From beginning to end he's there, towering far above everything, everyone. So spacious is he, so roomy, that everything of God finds its proper place in him without crowding. Not only that, but all the broken and dislocated pieces of the universe—people and things, animals and atoms—get properly fixed and fit together in vibrant harmonies, all because of his death, his blood that poured down from the cross."

The power of Christ's resurrection is enough not only to remake us, but also to remake every inch of the universe—mountains, rivers, plants, animals, stars, nebulae, quasars, and galaxies. Christ's redemptive work extends resurrection to the far reaches of the universe. This is a stunning affirmation of God's greatness. It should move our hearts to wonder and praise.

Eternal Promises

I heard a voice from heaven say, "Write: Blessed are the dead who die in the Lord from now on." "Yes," says the Spirit, "they will rest from their labor, for their deeds will follow them."

REVELATION 14:13

The fruit of the righteous is a tree of life.

PROVERBS 11:30

Heavenly Assignments

Anticipating eternal life as resurrected beings in a resurrected universe has present, practical implications. "Therefore [in light of our eventual resurrection], my dear brothers, stand firm. Let nothing move you. Always give yourselves fully to the work of the Lord, because you know that your labor in the Lord is not in vain" (1 Corinthians 15:58).

How do we know that our labor in the Lord is not in vain? Because of our bodily resurrection. Just as we will be carried over from the old world to the new, so will our labor. In a sense, not only our bodies but our service for Christ will be resurrected.

Our righteous works will follow us to Heaven (Revelation 14:13). Not only will some things that God has made survive his judgment, but so will some things *we* have done. Products of faithful lives will endure.

Eternal Promises

God was pleased to have all his fullness dwell in
[Christ], and through him to reconcile to himself all
things, whether things on earth or things in heaven, by
making peace through his blood, shed on the cross.

COLOSSIANS 1:19-20

The desert and the parched land will be glad;
   the wilderness will rejoice and blossom.
Like the crocus, it will burst into bloom;
   it will rejoice greatly and shout for joy....
They will see the glory of the LORD,
   the splendor of our God.

ISAIAH 35:1-2

Treasured Things in Heaven

If our bodies and the works of our hands that please God will be resurrected, why not a chair, cabinet, or wardrobe made by Jesus in his carpenter's shop in Nazareth? Couldn't God reassemble those molecules as easily as our own? What about things we made to God's glory? Could these be resurrected or reassembled?

Might Jesus resurrect a specific flower arrangement given to a sick person that prompted a spiritual turning point? Might he resurrect a song or book written to his glory? or a letter written to encourage a friend or stranger? or a blanket a grandmother made for her grandchild? or a baseball bat that a man handcrafted for his grandson's eleventh birthday?

Some may think it silly or sentimental to suppose that nature, animals, paintings, books, or a baseball bat might be resurrected, appearing to trivialize the coming resurrection. I would suggest that it does exactly the opposite: It *elevates* resurrection, emphasizing the power of Christ to radically renew not only mankind, but the entire fallen creation.

Eternal Promises

We are God's workmanship, created in Christ Jesus
to do good works, which God prepared in advance
for us to do.

EPHESIANS 2:10

A longing fulfilled is sweet to the soul.

PROVERBS 13:19

The Art on Heaven's Fridge

Because God will resurrect the earth itself, we know that the resurrection of the dead extends to things that are inanimate. Scripture is clear that in some form, at least, what's done on Earth to Christ's glory will survive. Our error has not been in overestimating the extent of God's redemption and resurrection but *underestimating* it.

Close your eyes and picture something special hanging on your living-room wall or posted on your refrigerator. You may see these things in Heaven, and not just in your memory. Picture the kinds of things done by his children that God, the ultimate father, would put on display. God rewards with permanency what is precious to his heart. What pleases him will not forever disappear.

If we understand the meaning of *resurrection*, it will revolutionize our thinking about the eternal Heaven. God, whose grace overflows, may be lavish in what he chooses to resurrect.

Eternal Promises

[Christ] did not enter by means of the blood of goats and calves; but he entered the Most Holy Place once for all by his own blood, having obtained eternal redemption.

HEBREWS 9:12

[Jesus Christ] died for us so that, whether we are awake or asleep, we may live together with him.

1 THESSALONIANS 5:10

Fully Alive, Fully Physical

Because ethereal notions of Heaven have largely gone unchallenged, we often think of Heaven as less real and less substantial than life here and now. (Hence, we don't think of Heaven as a place where people will hug, and certainly not in *these* bodies.) But in Heaven we won't be shadow people living in shadowlands—to borrow C. S. Lewis's imagery. Instead, we'll be fully alive and fully physical in a fully physical universe.

In one sense, we've never seen a friend's body as truly as we will see it in the eternal Heaven. We've never been hugged here as meaningfully as we'll be hugged there. And we've never known this earth to be all that we will then know it to be.

Jesus Christ died to secure for us a resurrected life on a resurrected Earth. Let's be careful that what we say about Heaven does justice to the greatness of Christ's redemptive work.

Eternal Promises

Your dead will live;
    their bodies will rise.
You who dwell in the dust,
    wake up and shout for joy.
Your dew is like the dew of the morning;
    the earth will give birth to her dead.

ISAIAH 26:19

Now in Christ Jesus you who once were far away have
been brought near through the blood of Christ.

EPHESIANS 2:13

On Earth as It Is in Heaven

The ancient Israelites' hope was that one day God would rule on Earth, removing sin, death, suffering, poverty, and heartache. They believed the Messiah would come and bring Heaven to Earth. He would make God's will be done on Earth as it is in Heaven—not only for their distant offspring but also for *themselves*. They longed for God's rule on Earth, not just for a hundred years or a thousand, but forever.

When we read passages about a future earthly kingdom in the Old Testament, we assume they don't refer to Heaven. But because God will dwell with his people on the New Earth, these Scripture passages *do* refer to Heaven. Just as Adam was made from the dust of the earth, we will be remade from the dust to which we returned at death. God's people are not looking for deliverance *from* Earth, but deliverance *on* Earth. That's exactly what we will find after our bodily resurrection.

Eternal Promises

The twelve gates were twelve pearls, each gate made of
a single pearl. The great street of the city was of pure
gold, like transparent glass.

REVELATION 21:21

Your gates will stay open around the clock
    to receive the wealth of many lands.
The kings of the world will be led as captives
    in a victory procession.

ISAIAH 60:11, NLT

Mission Accomplished

In Isaiah 11:1-10, we're told of the Messiah's mission to Earth: "He will defend the poor and the exploited. He will rule against the wicked and destroy them" (v. 4, NLT). With the lifting of the Curse, the Messiah will bring peace to the animal kingdom: "The wolf will live with the lamb, the leopard will lie down with the goat" (v. 6, NIV). Isaiah says there will be no harm or destruction in Jerusalem (v. 9). "The nations will rally to him [the Messiah]" (v. 10, NLT). His "place of rest will be glorious" (v. 10, NIV).

This will happen "down here" on Earth, in Jerusalem. Isaiah 60 speaks of the city gates always being open, because there are no longer any enemies. In words nearly identical to those of John concerning the New Earth (Revelation 21:24-26), it speaks of nations and kings bringing in their wealth. It tells of God's light replacing the sun's and promises that "your days of sorrow will end" (Isaiah 60:19-20)— two prophecies clearly fulfilled in Revelation.

Eternal Promises

[The angel said,] "I bring you good news of great joy that will be for all the people. Today in the town of David a Savior has been born to you; he is Christ the Lord."

LUKE 2:10-11

To us a child is born,
  to us a son is given,
  and the government will be on his shoulders.
And he will be called
  Wonderful Counselor, Mighty God,
  Everlasting Father, Prince of Peace.

ISAIAH 9:6

A King Who Will Reign Forever

The angel Gabriel promised Mary concerning Jesus, "The Lord God will give him the throne of his father David, and he will reign over the house of Jacob forever; his kingdom will never end" (Luke 1:32-33). David's throne is not in Heaven but on Earth. It is God's reign on Earth, not in Heaven, that is the focus of the unfolding drama of redemption. That earthly reign will be forever established on the New Earth.

God has a future plan for the earth and a future plan for Jerusalem. His plan involves an actual kingdom over which he and his people will reign—not merely for a thousand years but forever (Revelation 22:5). It will be the long-delayed but never-derailed fulfillment of God's command for mankind to exercise righteous dominion over the earth.

Eternal Promises

The kingdom of God is not a matter of eating and drinking, but of righteousness, peace and joy in the Holy Spirit.

ROMANS 14:17

You will go out in joy
and be led forth in peace;
the mountains and hills
will burst into song before you,
and all the trees of the field
will clap their hands.

ISAIAH 55:12

Shalom

God's people were right to expect the Messiah to bring an earthly kingdom. That's exactly what God promised: "All kings shall fall down before Him; all nations shall serve Him" (Psalm 72:11, NKJV). An explicitly messianic passage tells us, "His rule will extend from sea to sea and from the River to the ends of the earth" (Zechariah 9:10).

God promises that he has a great future in store for Jerusalem, in which, he says, "I will extend peace to her like a river, and the wealth of nations like a flooding stream" (Isaiah 66:12).

Every time Jewish people greet each other with *Shalom*, they express the God-given cry of the heart to live in a world where there's no sin, suffering, or death. There was once such a world, enjoyed by only two people and some animals. But there will again be such a world, enjoyed by all its inhabitants, including everyone who knows Christ.

Eternal Promises

Put on your garments of splendor,
    O Jerusalem, the holy city.
The uncircumcised and defiled
    will not enter you again.

ISAIAH 52:1

I will write on him [who overcomes] the name of my
God and the name of the city of my God, the new
Jerusalem, which is coming down out of heaven from
my God.

REVELATION 3:12

A Destination City

Isaiah 66 says that peace will come to Jerusalem and Jerusalem will become a center of all nations. " 'I . . . am about to come and gather all nations and tongues, and they will come and see my glory. . . . All mankind will come and bow down before me,' says the LORD" (Isaiah 66:18, 23).

This prophecy, like the others, is clearly fulfilled in the later chapters of Revelation. Jerusalem will again be a center of worship. Because this Jerusalem will reside on the New Earth, wouldn't we expect it to be called the New Jerusalem? That's exactly what it is called (Revelation 3:12; 21:2).

Scripture's repeated promises about land, peace, and the centrality of Jerusalem among all cities and nations will be fulfilled. On the New Earth the people of God will "possess the land *forever*" (Isaiah 60:21, emphasis added).

Eternal Promises

If anyone is in Christ, he is a new creation; the old has gone, the new has come!

2 CORINTHIANS 5:17

You were . . . buried with [Christ] in baptism and raised with him through your faith in the power of God, who raised him from the dead.

COLOSSIANS 2:11-12

Better than Old or New

The expression "Heaven and Earth" is a biblical designation for the entire universe. So when Revelation 21:1 speaks of "a new heaven and a new earth," it indicates a transformation of the entire universe. The Greek word *kainos*, translated "new," indicates that the earth God creates won't merely be new as opposed to old, but new in quality and superior in character.

Paul uses the same word, *kainos*, when he speaks of a believer becoming "a new creation" (2 Corinthians 5:17, NKJV). The New Earth will be the same as the old Earth, just as a new Christian is still the same person he was before. Changed? Yes. Better? Yes. But also the same.

As God may gather the scattered DNA and atoms and molecules of our bodies, he will regather all he needs of the scorched and disfigured Earth. As our old bodies will be raised to new bodies, so the old Earth will be raised to become the New Earth.

Eternal Promises

I press on to take hold of that for which Christ Jesus took hold of me.

PHILIPPIANS 3:12

You gave me life and showed me your unfailing love.

JOB 10:12, NLT

Familiar but So Much Better

As human beings, we long for home, even as we step out to explore undiscovered new frontiers. We long for the familiarity of the old, even as we crave the innovation of the new. Think of all the things we love that are new: moving into a new house; the smell of a new car; the feel of a new book; a new movie; a new song; the pleasure of a new friend; the enjoyment of a new pet; new presents on Christmas; welcoming a new child or grandchild; trying new foods. We love newness—yet in each case, what is new is attached to something familiar. We appreciate fresh and innovative variations on things that we already know and love. So when we hear that in Heaven we will have new bodies and live on a New Earth, that's how we should understand the word *new*—a restored and perfected version of our familiar bodies and our familiar Earth and our familiar relationships.

Eternal Promises

When the perishable has been clothed with the imperishable, and the mortal with immortality, then the saying that is written will come true: "Death has been swallowed up in victory." "Where, O death, is your victory? Where, O death, is your sting?" The sting of death is sin, and the power of sin is the law.

1 CORINTHIANS 15:54-56

When you were dead in your sins and in the uncircumcision of your sinful nature, God made you alive with Christ. He forgave us all our sins, having canceled the written code, with its regulations, that was against us and that stood opposed to us; he took it away, nailing it to the cross.

COLOSSIANS 2:13-14

Re-gifting the World

We want to live forever in a world with all the beauty and none of the ugliness—a world without sin, death, the Curse, and all the personal and relational problems and disappointments they create.

Understanding and anticipating the physical nature of the New Earth corrects a multitude of errors. This frees us to love the world that God has made, without guilt, while saying no to the world corrupted by our sin. God himself gave us the earth, gave us a *love* for the earth, and will delight to give us the New Earth.

Think for a moment what this will mean for Adam and Eve. When the New Earth comes down from Heaven, the rest of us will be going home, but Adam and Eve will be *coming* home. Only they will have experienced, at least to a degree, the treasure of an original, magnificent Earth that was lost and is now regained.

Eternal Promises

"Let us rejoice and be glad
    and give him glory!
For the wedding of the Lamb has come,
    and his bride has made herself ready.
Fine linen, bright and clean,
    was given her to wear."
(Fine linen stands for the righteous acts of the saints.)

REVELATION 19:7-8

The Spirit and the bride say, "Come!" And let him
who hears say, "Come!" Whoever is thirsty, let him
come; and whoever wishes, let him take the free gift
of the water of life.

REVELATION 22:17

Anticipating Our Bridegroom

The Bible portrays life in God's presence, in our resurrected bodies in a resurrected universe, as so exciting and compelling that even the youngest and healthiest of us should daydream about it. If we fall in love with the place and look forward to the future that God has for us, we'll fall more in love with God, and we'll be emboldened to follow him with greater resolve and perspective.

When we see Heaven for the first time with our own eyes, we'll know it's exactly where we belong. Thankfully, we don't have to wait until we die to learn about Heaven.

As a bride lives daily in anticipation of the bridegroom's arrival, coming to take her to the house he's built for her, we should think daily about Jesus—our Bridegroom—and about Heaven. A bride knows that she will live in the home the bridegroom has lovingly constructed with her in mind, where they'll joyfully live together forever.

Eternal Promises

Even the sparrow has found a home,
    and the swallow a nest for herself,
    where she may have her young—
a place near your altar,
    O LORD Almighty, my King and my God.
Blessed are those who dwell in your house;
    they are ever praising you.

PSALM 84:3-4

Anyone who has died has been freed from sin. Now if
we died with Christ, we believe that we will also live
with him.

ROMANS 6:7-8

Favorite and Cherished Things

When the Bible tells us that Heaven is our home, what meanings should we attach to the word *home*?

Familiarity is one. I have countless pleasurable memories from childhood. Even those who endured childhood traumas usually have some good memories too. When I go past my childhood home, I step back into a place inseparable from who I was and am, inseparable from my family and friends.

A place with loved ones—that's a central quality of home.

Heaven will be just like that. We'll be with people we love, and we'll love no one more than Jesus, who purchased with his own blood the real estate of the New Earth. It won't be long before we settle in there. Because we've already lived on Earth, I think it will seem from the first that we're coming home. Because we once lived on Earth, the New Earth will strike us as very familiar.

Eternal Promises

[Jesus said,] "In my Father's house are many rooms; if it were not so, I would have told you. I am going there to prepare a place for you."

JOHN 14:2

One thing I ask of the LORD,
    this is what I seek:
that I may dwell in the house of the LORD
    all the days of my life.

PSALM 27:4

Custom Made for Us

Home is a place where we fit right in. It's the place
we were made for. Most houses we live in on Earth
weren't really made just for us. But the New Earth
will be. What kind of a place can we expect our Lord
to have prepared for us? Because he isn't limited and
he loves us even more than we love our children,
I think we can expect to find the best place ever made
by anyone, for anyone, in the history of the universe.
The God who commends hospitality will not be out-
done in his hospitality to us. Jesus is the carpenter
from Nazareth. He knows how to build. He's had
experience building entire worlds (billions of them,
throughout the universe). He's going to remodel the
old Earth on a grand scale. How great will be the resurrected planet that he calls the New Earth—the one
he says will be our home . . . and *his*.

Eternal Promises

I saw a new heaven and a new earth, for the old heaven and the old earth had disappeared.

REVELATION 21:1, NLT

Men will see the Son of Man coming in clouds with great power and glory. And he will send his angels and gather his elect from the four winds, from the ends of the earth to the ends of the heavens.

MARK 13:26-27

The Complete Package

By calling the New Earth *Earth*, God emphatically tells us it will be earthly, and thus familiar. The New Earth will be a far better version of the old Earth.

The word *new* is an adjective describing a noun. The noun is the main thing. A new car is first and foremost a car. A new body is mainly a body. A New Earth is mainly an Earth.

The New Earth will not be a non-Earth but a real Earth. The Earth spoken of in Scripture is the Earth we know—with dirt, water, rocks, trees, flowers, animals, people, and a variety of natural wonders. An Earth without these would not be Earth.

The Greek word translated "earth" is *ge*, from which we get "geology." *Ge* connotes physicality, an earthly realm where there are physical human beings, animals, vegetation, and natural resources.

Mankind and Earth are inseparable. Without people, the earth would be incomplete. Without the earth, people would be incomplete.

Eternal Promises

The Word became flesh and made his dwelling among us. We have seen his glory, the glory of the One and Only, who came from the Father, full of grace and truth.

JOHN 1:14

Since [God's] children have flesh and blood, [Jesus] too shared in their humanity so that by his death he might destroy him who holds the power of death— that is, the devil—and free those who all their lives were held in slavery by their fear of death.

HEBREWS 2:14

The Transparent Becomes Immanent

Scripture portrays God as holy and transcendent. Because Heaven is his dwelling place, it seems inappropriate to think of Heaven in earthly terms. But even before Christ's incarnation, God came to the Garden to walk with Adam and Eve. And Christ's incarnation and resurrection took it much further—one member of the transcendent triune God became *permanently* immanent. Jesus is in physical form, in a human resurrection body, for all eternity. (He may choose to exercise his divine omnipresence in a way we can't comprehend, but Jesus the risen Savior will not cease to be the eternal God-man.) His marriage to us is not an unequal yoke of a spiritual God to physical people—not only are we also spiritual, but Jesus, by incarnation and resurrection, is also physical.

Before the Incarnation, Heaven was transcendent. By virtue of the Incarnation, Heaven became immanent. The coming New Earth will be God's dwelling place, as pure and holy as Heaven has ever been.

Eternal Promises

The highest heavens belong to the LORD,
   but the earth he has given to man.

PSALM 115:16

At that time I will gather you;
   at that time I will bring you home.
I will give you honor and praise
   among all the peoples of the earth.

ZEPHANIAH 3:20

We're Living the Preview

Do you recall a time when you were away from your earthly home and desperately missed it? Maybe it was when you were off at college or in the military or traveling extensively overseas or needed to move because of a job. Do you remember how your heart ached for home? That's how we should feel about Heaven. We are a displaced people, longing for our home.

A Christian I met in passing once told me it troubled him that he really didn't long for Heaven. Instead, he yearned for an Earth that was like God meant it to be. In fact, the very place he's always longed for, an Earth where God was fully glorified, is the place where he will live forever.

What we love about this life are the things that resonate with the life we were made for. The things we love are not merely the best this life has to offer—they are previews of the greater life to come.

Eternal Promises

When Christ, who is your life, appears, then you also will appear with him in glory.

COLOSSIANS 3:4

[Jesus said,] "Father, I want those you have given me to be with me where I am, and to see my glory, the glory you have given me because you loved me before the creation of the world."

JOHN 17:24

Basking in His Presence

Our longing for Heaven is a longing for God—
a longing that involves not only our inner beings,
but our bodies as well. Being with God is the heart
and soul of Heaven. Every other heavenly pleasure
will derive from and be secondary to his presence.
God's greatest gift to us is, and always will be,
himself.

Ancient theologians often spoke of the "beatific
vision." The term comes from three Latin words that
together mean "a happy-making sight." The sight they
spoke of was God. Revelation 22:4 says of God's servants on the New Earth, "They will see his face."

The New Testament says that God "lives in
unapproachable light, whom no one has seen or can
see" (1 Timothy 6:16). It's only because we'll be fully
righteous in Christ, completely sinless, that we'll
be able to see God and live. The blood of Jesus has
bought us full access to God's throne room and his
Most Holy Place.

Eternal Promises

In Christ all the fullness of the Deity lives in bodily form, and you have been given fullness in Christ, who is the head over every power and authority.

COLOSSIANS 2:9-10

John saw Jesus coming toward him and said, "Look, the Lamb of God, who takes away the sin of the world! This is the one I meant when I said, 'A man who comes after me has surpassed me because he was before me.'"

JOHN 1:29-30

Face-to-Face with Our Redeemer

Will the Christ we worship in Heaven as God also be a man? Yes. "Jesus Christ is the same yesterday [when he lived on Earth], today [when he lives in the present Heaven], and forever [when he will live on the New Earth, in the eternal Heaven]" (Hebrews 13:8, NLT). Christ was and is and will be always a man *and* God. When Christ died, he might have appeared to shed his humanity; but when he rose in an indestructible body, he declared his permanent identity as the God-man.

Job, in his anguish, cried out in a vision of striking clarity: "I know that my Redeemer lives, and that in the end he will stand upon the earth. And after my skin has been destroyed, yet in my flesh I will see God; I myself will see him with my own eyes—I, and not another. How my heart yearns within me!" (Job 19:25-27). The anticipation of seeing God face-to-face, in our resurrected bodies, is heartfelt and ancient.

Eternal Promises

Blessed are the pure in heart,
    for they will see God.

MATTHEW 5:8

Jesus [said,] "You will be with me in paradise."

LUKE 23:43

Truly Seeing for the First Time

We need not wait till the New Earth to catch glimpses
of God. We're told his "invisible qualities" can be
"clearly seen" in "what has been made" (Romans 1:20).
Consider the trees, flowers, sun, rain, and the people
around you. Yes, there's devastation all around us
and within us. Eden has been trampled, burned, and
savaged. Yet the stars in the sky nevertheless declare
God's glory (Psalm 19:1), as do animals, art, and music.
One day both we and the universe will be forever
cured of sin. In that day, *we will see God.*

In Heaven, the barriers between redeemed human
beings and God will forever be gone. To look into
God's eyes will be to see what we've always longed to
see: the person who made us for his own good pleasure.
Seeing God will be like seeing . . . for the first time. He
will be the lens through which we see everything else—
people, ourselves, and the events of this life.

Eternal Promises

Command those who are rich in this present world not to be arrogant nor to put their hope in wealth, which is so uncertain, but to put their hope in God, who richly provides us with everything for our enjoyment.

1 TIMOTHY 6:17

[God] did not spare his own Son, but gave him up for us all—how will he not also, along with him, graciously give us all things?

ROMANS 8:32

God's Greatest Gift

God is the ultimate source of joy, and because all secondary joys emanate from him, to love secondary joys on Earth *can be*—and in Heaven *always will be*—to love God, their source.

Flowers are beautiful for one reason— God is beautiful. Rainbows are stunning because God is stunning. Puppies are delightful because God is delightful. Sports are fun because God is fun. Study is rewarding because God is rewarding. Work is fulfilling because God is fulfilling.

God is a lavish giver. The God who gave us his Son delights to graciously give us "all things." These "all things" are in addition to Christ, but they are never *instead* of him— they come, Scripture tells us, "along with him." If we didn't have Christ, we would have nothing. But because we have Christ, we have everything. Hence, we can enjoy the people and things God has made, and in the process enjoy the God who designed and provided them for his pleasure and ours.

Eternal Promises

Give thanks to the LORD for his unfailing love
    and his wonderful deeds for men,
for he satisfies the thirsty
    and fills the hungry with good things.

PSALM 107:8-9

Jesus [said,] "I am the bread of life. He who comes to
me will never go hungry, and he who believes in me
will never be thirsty."

JOHN 6:35

Abundance without End

God's creatures find joy in feasting on Heaven's abundance and drinking deeply of his delights: "You feed them from the abundance of your own house, letting them drink from your river of delights. For you are the fountain of life, the light by which we see" (Psalm 36:8-9, NLT). This abundance and the river of delights flow from and are completely dependent on their source: God. He alone is the fountain of life, and without him there could be neither life nor joy, neither abundance nor delights.

God doesn't want to be replaced or depreciated. He wants to be recognized as the source of all our joys, and he wants us to draw closer to him through partaking of his creation. My taking pleasure in a good meal or a good book is taking pleasure in God. It's not a substitute for God, nor is it a distraction from him. It's what I was made for.

Eternal Promises

The Son is the radiance of God's glory and the exact representation of his being, sustaining all things by his powerful word. After he had provided purification for sins, he sat down at the right hand of the Majesty in heaven.

HEBREWS 1:3

Everything he does reveals his glory and majesty.

PSALM 111:3, NLT

Endless Exploration

In Jeremiah 31:34, God describes his future Kingdom: "No longer will a man teach his neighbor, or a man his brother, saying, 'Know the LORD,' because they will all know me, from the least of them to the greatest." There will always be more to see when we look at God, because his infinite character can never be exhausted. We could—and will—spend countless millennia exploring the depths of God's being. This is the magnificence of God and the wonder of Heaven.

We will spend eternity worshiping, exploring, and serving God, seeing his magnificent beauty in everything and everyone around us. In the new universe, as we study nature, as we pursue science and mathematics and every realm of knowledge, we'll see God in everything, for he's behind it all.

And yet, all our explorations and adventures and projects in the eternal Heaven—and I believe there will be many—will pale in comparison to the wonder of seeing God face-to-face.

Eternal Promises

My dwelling place will be with them; I will be their God, and they will be my people.

EZEKIEL 37:27

"As the new heavens and the new earth that I make will endure before me," declares the LORD, "so will your name and descendants endure."

ISAIAH 66:22

Heaven on Earth

On the New Earth, God and mankind will live together forever in the same home.

The marriage of the God of Heaven with the people of Earth will bring the marriage of Heaven and Earth. There will not be two universes—one the primary home of God and angels, the other the primary home of humanity. Nothing will separate us from God, and nothing will separate Earth and Heaven. Once God and mankind dwell together, there will be no difference between Heaven and Earth. Earth will become Heaven—and it will truly be Heaven on Earth. The New Earth will be God's locus, his dwelling place. I do not hesitate to call the New Earth "Heaven," for where God makes his home is Heaven. The purpose of God will at last be achieved: "To bring all things in heaven and on earth together under one head, even Christ" (Ephesians 1:10).

Eternal Promises

Now the dwelling of God is with men, and he will live with them. They will be his people, and God himself will be with them and be their God.

REVELATION 21:3

Forgetting what is behind and straining toward what is ahead, I press on toward the goal to win the prize for which God has called me heavenward in Christ Jesus.

PHILIPPIANS 3:13-14

Heaven's Greatest Prize

Revelation 21:3 says, "God himself will be with them." Why does it emphatically say God *himself*? Because God won't merely send us a delegate. He will actually come to live among us on the New Earth.

God's glory will be the air we breathe, and we'll always breathe deeper to gain more of it. In the new universe, we'll never be able to travel far enough to leave God's presence. If we could, we'd never want to. However great the wonders of Heaven, God himself is Heaven's greatest prize.

In Heaven we'll no longer question God's goodness; we'll see it, savor it, enjoy it, and declare it to our companions. Surely we will wonder how we ever could have doubted his goodness. For then our faith will be sight—*we shall see God.*

In *The Happiness of Heaven*, published in 1871, Father J. Boudreau writes, "The beatitude of Heaven consists essentially in the vision, love, and enjoyment of God himself."[7]

Eternal Promises

The LORD has chosen Zion,
    he has desired it for his dwelling:
"This is my resting place for ever and ever;
    here I will sit enthroned, for I have desired it—
I will bless her with abundant provisions."

PSALM 132:13-15

[Jesus said,] "I will come back and take you to be with
me that you also may be where I am."

JOHN 14:3

The Ultimate Relocation

When God comes to dwell with us on Earth, he will also bring with him the New Jerusalem, an entire city of people, structures, streets, walls, rivers, and trees that is now in the present, intermediate Heaven. God will relocate an entire city—Heaven's capital city, the New Jerusalem—from Heaven to Earth. It's a vast complex containing, perhaps, hundreds of millions of residences. He will bring with it Heaven's human inhabitants and angels as well.

It appears that God has already fashioned the New Jerusalem: "He has prepared a city for them" (Hebrews 11:16). It doesn't say that God *will* prepare a city or even that he *is preparing* it, but that he *has* prepared it. It's possible that those in the present Heaven are already living in it. Or it may be set aside, awaiting simultaneous habitation by *all* its occupants when transferred to the New Earth. Imagine the thrill of beholding and exploring God's city together!

Eternal Promises

Great is the LORD in Zion;
    he is exalted over all the nations.
Let them praise your great and awesome name—
    he is holy.

PSALM 99:2-3

Blessed are those who . . . may go through the gates
into the city.

REVELATION 22:14

Total Access

To be with God—to know him, to see him—is the central, irreducible draw of Heaven.

The presence of God is the essence of Heaven (just as the absence of God is the essence of Hell). Because God is beautiful beyond measure, if we knew nothing more than that Heaven was God's dwelling place, it would be more than enough. The best part of life on the New Earth will be enjoying God's presence, having him actually dwell among us (Revelation 21:3-4). Just as the Holy of Holies contained the dazzling presence of God in ancient Israel, so will the New Jerusalem contain his presence—but on a much larger scale—on the New Earth.

In the New Jerusalem, there will be no temple (Revelation 21:22). Heaven's greatest miracle will be our access to God. Everyone will be allowed unimpeded access into God's presence; we will be able to come physically, through wide open gates, to God's throne.

Eternal Promises

Your attitude should be the same as that of
    Christ Jesus:
Who, being in very nature God,
    did not consider equality with God something
      to be grasped,
but made himself nothing. . . .
And being found in appearance as a man,
    he humbled himself
    and became obedient to death—
      even death on a cross!
Therefore God exalted him to the highest place
    and gave him the name that is above every name,
that at the name of Jesus every knee should bow,
    in heaven and on earth and under the earth,
and every tongue confess that Jesus Christ is Lord,
    to the glory of God the Father.

PHILIPPIANS 2:5-11

I will praise you, O Lord my God, with all my heart;
    I will glorify your name forever.
For great is your love toward me;
    you have delivered me from the depths of the grave.

PSALM 86:12-13

Sharing His Glory

When Jesus prays that we will be with him in Heaven, he explains why: "Father, I want those you have given me to be with me where I am, and *to see my glory*, the glory you have given me because you loved me before the creation of the world" (John 17:24, emphasis added). When we accomplish something, we want to share it with those closest to us. Likewise, Jesus wants to share with us his glory—his person and his accomplishments. There's no contradiction between Christ acting for his glory and for our good. The two are synonymous. Our greatest pleasure, our greatest satisfaction, is to behold his glory.

Christ's desire for us to see his glory should touch us deeply. What an unexpected compliment that the Creator of the universe has gone to such great lengths, at such sacrifice, to prepare a place for us where we can behold and participate in his glory.

Eternal Promises

I will live with them and walk among them, and I will be their God, and they will be my people.

2 CORINTHIANS 6:16

Look, he is coming with the clouds,
    and every eye will see him,
even those who pierced him;
    and all the peoples of the earth will mourn
        because of him.
                            So shall it be! Amen.

REVELATION 1:7

Here, There, and Everywhere

When Christ returns "every eye will see him" (Revelation 1:7). How is that physically possible? Will he be in more than one place at one time?

If God took on human form any number of times, as recorded in Scripture, couldn't Christ choose to take on a form to manifest himself to us at a distant place? Might Jesus appear to us and walk with us in a temporary but tangible form that is an expression of his real body? Or might the one body of Jesus be simultaneously present with his people in a million places?

Might we walk with Jesus (not just spiritually, but also physically) while millions of others are also walking with him? Might we not be able to touch his hand or embrace him or spend a long afternoon privately conversing with him—not just with his spirit, but his whole person? It may defy our logic, but God is capable of doing far more than we imagine.

Eternal Promises

I know that my Redeemer lives,
    and that in the end he will stand upon the earth.

JOB 19:25

Dear brothers and sisters, work hard to prove that you
really are among those God has called and chosen. . . .
Then God will give you a grand entrance into the
eternal Kingdom of our Lord and Savior Jesus Christ.

2 PETER 1:10-11, NLT

Dinner with Jesus

If you had the opportunity to spend the evening with any person who's ever lived, whom would you choose? Probably someone fascinating, knowledgeable, and accomplished. Or perhaps you'd choose someone beautiful and talented.

Is Jesus the first person you would choose? Who is more beautiful, talented, knowledgeable, fascinating, and interesting than he?

The good news is, *he chose you.* If you're a Christian, you'll be with him for eternity and enjoy endless fascinating conversations and experiences. Incredibly, he'll also enjoy your company and mine. After all, he paid the ultimate price just so he could have us over to his place for eternity.

Most of us would love to spend the evening with a great author, musician, artist, or head of state. God is the master artist who created the universe, the inventor of music, the author and main character of the unfolding drama of redemption. All that is admirable and fascinating in human beings comes from their creator.

Eternal Promises

Whatever is true, whatever is noble, whatever is right, whatever is pure, whatever is lovely, whatever is admirable—if anything is excellent or praiseworthy—think about such things.

PHILIPPIANS 4:8

Here we do not have an enduring city, but we are looking for the city that is to come. Through Jesus, therefore, let us continually offer to God a sacrifice of praise—the fruit of lips that confess his name.

HEBREWS 13:14-15

The Big Reveal

"Since, then, you have been raised with Christ, set your hearts on things above, where Christ is seated at the right hand of God. Set your minds on things above, not on earthly things. For you died, and *your life is now hidden with Christ in God.* When Christ, who is your life, appears, then you also will appear with him in glory" (Colossians 3:1-4, emphasis added).

Our intimate link with Christ in his redemptive work makes us inseparable from him, even now. As we walk with him and commune with him in this world, we experience a faint foretaste of Heaven's delights and wonders.

Though it's true that Christ is with us and within us while we're on Earth, it also works in the other direction—we're united with Christ, so much so that we are seated with him in Heaven: "God raised us up with Christ and seated us with him in the heavenly realms in Christ Jesus" (Ephesians 2:6).

Eternal Promises

[Jesus said,] "Whoever hears my word and believes him who sent me has eternal life and will not be condemned; he has crossed over from death to life."

JOHN 5:24

See that what you have heard from the beginning remains in you. If it does, you also will remain in the Son and in the Father. And this is what he promised us—even eternal life.

1 JOHN 2:24-25

Be Heavenly Minded

In a metaphysical sense, we've already entered Heaven's community. By seeing ourselves as part of the heavenly society, we can learn to rejoice *now* in what Heaven's residents rejoice in. They rejoice in God, his glory, his grace, and his beauty. They rejoice in repentant sinners, the saints' faithfulness and Christlikeness, and the beauty of God's creation. They rejoice in the ultimate triumph of God's Kingdom and the coming judgment of sin.

Heaven, then, isn't only our future home. It's our home already, waiting over the next hill. If we really grasp this truth, it will have a profound effect on our holiness. No wonder the devil is so intent on keeping us from grasping our standing in Christ—for if we see ourselves in Heaven with Christ, we'll be drawn to worship and serve him here and now, creating ripples in Heaven's waters that will extend outward for all eternity.

Eternal Promises

O LORD, our Lord,
    how majestic is your name in all the earth!
You have set your glory
    above the heavens.

PSALM 8:1

LORD, you have assigned me my portion and my
    cup. . . .
The boundary lines have fallen for me in pleasant
    places;
    surely I have a delightful inheritance.

PSALM 16:5-6

Bored? Impossible!

Have you ever—in prayer or corporate worship or during a walk on the beach—for a few moments experienced the very presence of God? It's a tantalizing encounter, yet for most of us it tends to disappear quickly in the distractions of life. What will it be like to behold God's face and never be distracted by lesser things?

God is anything *but* boring. Seeing God will be dynamic, not static. It will mean exploring new beauties, unfolding new mysteries—forever. We'll explore God's being, an experience delightful beyond comprehension. The sense of wide-eyed wonder we see among Heaven's inhabitants in Revelation 4–5 suggests an ever-deepening appreciation of God's greatness. That isn't all there is to Heaven, but if it were, it would be more than enough.

In Heaven, we'll be at home with the God we love and who loves us wholeheartedly. Lovers don't bore each other. People who love God could never be bored in his presence.

Eternal Promises

Praise the LORD.
Praise God in his sanctuary;
    praise him in his mighty heavens.
Praise him for his acts of power;
    praise him for his surpassing greatness.

PSALM 150:1-2

In that day they will say,
"Surely this is our God;
    we trusted in him, and he saved us.
This is the LORD, we trusted in him;
    let us rejoice and be glad in his salvation."

ISAIAH 25:9

The Ultimate Worship Experience

Most people know that we'll worship God in Heaven. Multitudes of God's people—of every nation, tribe, people, and language—will gather to sing praise to God for his greatness, wisdom, power, grace, and mighty work of redemption (Revelation 5:13-14). Overwhelmed by his magnificence, we will fall on our faces in unrestrained happiness and say, "Praise and glory and wisdom and thanks and honor and power and strength be to our God for ever and ever. Amen!" (Revelation 7:9-12).

As Christians, we have the ultimate reason to celebrate—our relationship with Jesus and the promise of Heaven. Does this excite you? If it doesn't, you're not thinking correctly.

Will we always be engaged in worship? All that we do will be an act of worship. We'll enjoy full and unbroken fellowship with Christ. At times this will crescendo into greater heights of praise as we assemble with the multitudes who are also worshiping him.

Eternal Promises

My lips will shout for joy
    when I sing praise to you—
    I, whom you have redeemed.

PSALM 71:23

Since we are receiving a kingdom that cannot be
shaken, let us be thankful, and so worship God
acceptably with reverence and awe.

HEBREWS 12:28

Getting to Know Him

In Heaven, we'll never lose our fascination for God as we get to know him better. The thrill of knowing him will never subside. The desire to know him better will motivate everything we do.

But we can never get enough of God. There's no end to what he knows, no end to what he can do, no end to who he is. He is mesmerizing to the depths of his being, and those depths will never be exhausted.

The world is full of praise-prompters—the New Earth will overflow with them. If you've ever had a taste of true worship, you crave *more* of it, never less.

Has someone ever done something for you that makes you so grateful that you just can't stop saying thank you? This is how we should feel about God.

In Heaven, worshiping God won't be restricted to a certain time. It will permeate our lives, energize our bodies, and fuel our imaginations.

Eternal Promises

"Because he loves me," says the LORD, "I will
      rescue him;
   I will protect him, for he acknowledges my
      name. . . .
With long life will I satisfy him
   and show him my salvation."

PSALM 91:14, 16

Your Maker is your husband—
   the LORD Almighty is his name—
the Holy One of Israel is your Redeemer;
   he is called the God of all the earth.

ISAIAH 54:5

Cinderella's Rescue

Jesus called his disciples *friends* (John 15:15). He likewise regards us with deep affection. Good friendship is characterized by growth. Friendship with the God of Heaven has the most room for growth because of his inexhaustible greatness. Yet our relationship with Christ goes even beyond friendship.

"Blessed are those who are invited to the wedding supper of the Lamb!" (Revelation 19:9). It's amazing enough that we'll be invited to the King's wedding. What's beyond amazing is that we'll be his bride. There is an intimacy between husband and wife that includes close friendship yet also transcends it.

The return of Christ will signal not only the Father rescuing his children but also the Bridegroom rescuing his bride. As the church, we're part of the ultimate Cinderella story—rescued from a home where we labor, often without appreciation or reward. One day we'll be taken into the arms of the Prince and whisked away to live in his palace . . . forever!

Eternal Promises

O God, you are my God,
    earnestly I seek you;
my soul thirsts for you,
    my body longs for you.

PSALM 63:1

He who builds his lofty palace in the heavens
    and sets its foundation on the earth,
who calls for the waters of the sea
    and pours them out over the face of the land—
    the LORD is his name.

AMOS 9:6

More than Ever

God has made himself closely identified with Heaven. It's his place; *his* idea, not ours.

So, thinking about Heaven should be viewed as a *means* of knowing God. The infinite God reveals himself to us in tangible, finite expressions. Next to the incarnate Christ, Heaven will tell us more about God than anything else. Some people have told me, "I just want to be with Jesus—I don't care if Heaven's a shack." Well, Jesus cares. He *wants* us to anticipate Heaven and enjoy the magnificence of it. After preparing a place just for us, he wants us to be captivated by its beauty, not to say, "Who cares? I'd be just as happy in an old shack."

Every thought of Heaven should move our hearts toward God, just as every thought of God will move our hearts toward Heaven. To do one is to do the other. Heaven will not be an idol that competes with God but a lens by which we see God.

Those who love God should think more often of Heaven, not less.

Eternal Promises

Arise, shine, for [Zion's] light has come,
    and the glory of the LORD rises upon you. . . .
Nations will come to your light,
    and kings to the brightness of your dawn.
Lift up your eyes and look about you:
    All assemble and come to you;
your sons come from afar,
    and your daughters are carried on the arm.

ISAIAH 60:1, 3-4

We are heirs—heirs of God and co-heirs with Christ,
if indeed we share in his sufferings in order that we
may also share in his glory.

ROMANS 8:17

Pilgrims in the Promised Land

We are pilgrims on this earth that is passing away, but eventually we'll be pioneers and settlers on the New Earth.

The theme that Earth belongs to God and his people is carried throughout Psalms, Proverbs, and Isaiah. The Old Testament is filled with the idea of place, earth, land. Earth is the place of all mankind; Israel, especially Jerusalem, is the place of God's covenant people.

"If you belong to Christ, then you are Abraham's seed, and heirs according to the promise" (Galatians 3:29). New-covenant Christians, not just Israel, are heirs of the promises made to Abraham—and these promises center on possessing the land.

Inheritance typically involves land, a place lived on and managed by human beings. After our bodily resurrection, we will receive a physical inheritance. The New Earth is the ultimate Promised Land, the eternal Holy Land in which all God's people will dwell.

Eternal Promises

I say to myself, "The LORD is my portion;
    therefore I will wait for him."

LAMENTATIONS 3:24

[My people] . . . will inherit a double portion in
    their land,
    and everlasting joy will be theirs.

ISAIAH 61:7

God's Stewards in the Family Business

God is the sovereign ruler of the universe, yet he chooses not to rule the universe alone. He delegates responsibilities to angels, who exist in a hierarchy of command under Michael the archangel (Jude 1:9; Revelation 12:7). God made human beings in his image, as creators and rulers, to carry out his divine will. He does not grudgingly pass on to us management responsibilities. He delights to entrust Earth's rule to us. He has uniquely created and gifted us to handle such responsibilities and to find joy in them.

We've been born into the family of an incredibly wealthy landowner. There's not a millimeter of cosmic geography that doesn't belong to him, and by extension to his children, his heirs. Our Father has a family business that stretches across the whole universe. He entrusts to us management of the family business, and that's what we'll do for eternity: manage God's assets and rule his universe, representing him as his image-bearers, children, and ambassadors.

Eternal Promises

The nations will walk by its light, and the kings of the earth will bring their splendor into it [the New Jerusalem]. On no day will its gates ever be shut. . . . The glory and honor of the nations will be brought into it.

REVELATION 21:24-26

Of the increase of his government and peace
    there will be no end.
He will reign on David's throne
    and over his kingdom,
establishing and upholding it
    with justice and righteousness
    from that time on and forever.
The zeal of the LORD Almighty
    will accomplish this.

ISAIAH 9:7

His Plan Comes Full Circle

The events of human history aren't meaningless. Rather, they are heading toward the fulfillment of a divine plan, involving a New Earth with culture and citizens that glorify God.

Consider this prophetic statement: "The kingdom of the world has become the kingdom of our Lord and of his Christ, and he will reign for ever and ever" (Revelation 11:15). It doesn't say that Christ will destroy this world's kingdom. It doesn't even say he'll replace this world's kingdom. No, the kingdom of this world will actually *become* the Kingdom of Christ. God won't obliterate earthly kingdoms but will *transform them into his own.* And it's that new earthly kingdom (joined then to God's heavenly Kingdom) over which "he will reign for ever and ever."

This is a revolutionary viewpoint, in stark contrast to the prevalent myth that God's Kingdom will demolish and replace the kingdoms of Earth rather than cleanse, redeem, and resurrect them into his eternal Kingdom.

Eternal Promises

We have different gifts, according to the grace given us.

ROMANS 12:6

[The master said], "I tell you that to everyone who has, more will be given, but as for the one who has nothing, even what he has will be taken away."

LUKE 19:26

Faithful Service Rewarded

All of us will have some responsibility on the New Earth in which we serve God. Scripture teaches that our service for him now on Earth will be evaluated to help determine how we'll serve him on the New Earth. The humble servant will be put in charge of much, whereas the one who lords it over others in the present world will have power taken away: "For everyone who exalts himself will be humbled, and he who humbles himself will be exalted" (Luke 14:11). If we serve faithfully on the present Earth, God will give us permanent management positions on the New Earth. "Whoever can be trusted with very little can also be trusted with much" (Luke 16:10). The Owner has his eye on us—if we prove faithful, he'll be pleased to entrust more to us.

If God wants us to do something, we'll be wired and equipped to do it. Our service will not only bring him glory but also bring us joy.

Eternal Promises

Rejoice in the Lord always.

PHILIPPIANS 4:4

I will be glad and rejoice in you;
    I will sing praise to your name, O Most High.

PSALM 9:2

Whoever wants to become great among you must be
your servant, and whoever wants to be first must be
slave of all. For even the Son of Man did not come to
be served, but to serve, and to give his life as a ransom
for many.

MARK 10:43-45

The Master's Joy

The Master will say, "Well done, good and faithful servant. You have been faithful over a little; I will set you over much. Enter into the joy of your master" (Matthew 25:23, ESV).

The idea of entering into the Master's joy is a telling picture of Heaven. It's not simply that being with the Master produces joy in us, though certainly it will. Rather, it's that our Master himself is joyful. He takes joy in himself, in his children, and in his creation. His joy is contagious. Once we're liberated from the sin that blocks us from God's joy and our own, we'll enter into his joy. Joy will be the very air we breathe. The Lord is inexhaustible—therefore his joy is inexhaustible.

God is grooming us for leadership. He's watching to see how we demonstrate our faithfulness. He does that through his apprenticeship program, one that prepares us for Heaven. Christ is not simply preparing a place for us; he is preparing us for that place.

Eternal Promises

"Has not my hand made all these things,
    and so they came into being?"

declares the LORD.

"This is the one I esteem:
    he who is humble and contrite in spirit,
    and trembles at my word."

ISAIAH 66:2

At the renewal of all things . . . many who are first will
be last, and many who are last will be first.

MATTHEW 19:28, 30

The Meek Will Inherit the Earth

Daniel 7:18 explicitly reveals that "the saints of the Most High will receive the kingdom and will possess it forever." What is "the kingdom"? Earth.

Earth is unique. It's the one planet—perhaps among billions—where God chose to act out the unfolding drama of redemption and reveal the wonders of his grace. It's on the New Earth, the capital planet of the new universe, that he will establish an eternal Kingdom.

Daniel 7:21-22 says that an earthly ruler "was waging war against the saints and defeating them, *until* the Ancient of Days came and pronounced judgment in favor of the saints of the Most High, and the time came when they possessed the kingdom" (emphasis added).

The same earthly kingdoms ruled by ungodly human beings will ultimately be ruled by godly human beings. Christ's promise wasn't figurative—the meek really *will* inherit the earth (Matthew 5:5). And they will rule what they inherit.

Eternal Promises

How many are your works, O LORD!
    In wisdom you made them all;
        the earth is full of your creatures. . . .
May the glory of the LORD endure forever;
    may the LORD rejoice in his works.

PSALM 104:24, 31

They will be called the Holy People,
    the Redeemed of the LORD;
and you will be called Sought After,
    the City No Longer Deserted.

ISAIAH 62:12

Nothing Lost, Everything Gained

We've never seen men and women as they were intended to be. We've never seen animals the way they were before the Fall. We see only marred remnants of what once was.

Likewise, we've never seen nature unchained and undiminished. We've only seen it cursed and decaying. Yet even now we see a great deal that pleases and excites us, moving our hearts to worship.

If the "wrong side" of Heaven can be so beautiful, what will the right side look like? What will Earth look like when it's resurrected and made new, restored to the original? What lies in store for us is what we have seen only in diminished glimpses.

The earthly beauty we now see won't be lost. We won't *trade* Earth's beauty for Heaven's but *retain* Earth's beauty and *gain* even deeper beauty. As we will live forever with the people of this world—redeemed—we will enjoy forever the beauties of this world—redeemed.

Eternal Promises

The LORD will surely comfort Zion
    and will look with compassion on all her ruins;
he will make her deserts like Eden,
    her wastelands like the garden of the LORD.
Joy and gladness will be found in her,
    thanksgiving and the sound of singing.

ISAIAH 51:3

See, I am doing a new thing! . . .
I am making a way in the desert. . . .
I provide water in the desert
    and streams in the wasteland,
to give drink to my people, my chosen.

ISAIAH 43:19-20

More Wonderful Than We Remember

Our world is a copy of something that once was, Eden, and yet will be, the New Earth. All of the old Earth that matters will be drawn into Heaven, to be part of the New Earth.

On the New Earth we will see the *real* Earth, which includes the good things not only of God's natural creation but also of mankind's creative expression to God's glory. On the New Earth, no good thing will be destroyed.

Everything changes when we grasp that all we love about the old Earth will be ours on the New Earth—either in the same form or another. Once we understand this, we won't regret leaving all the wonders of the world we've seen or mourn not having seen its countless other wonders. Why? Because *we will yet be able to see them.*

God is no more done with the earth than he's done with us.

Eternal Promises

You [Zion] will be called by a new name
    that the mouth of the LORD will bestow.
You will be a crown of splendor in the LORD's hand,
    a royal diadem in the hand of your God.

ISAIAH 62:2-3

[God] spreads out the northern skies over
        empty space;
    he suspends the earth over nothing. . . .
He marks out the horizon on the face of the waters
    for a boundary between light and darkness. . . .
By his breath the skies became fair.

JOB 26:7, 10, 13

New Discoveries

We were *made* to be seekers and explorers. As we seek and explore God's creation, we'll grow in our knowledge of God, becoming increasingly motivated to explore the wonders of God himself.

The demands and distractions of our present life teach us to set aside or stifle our longing to explore, yet it still surfaces. On the New Earth, that desire won't be thwarted or trumped by pragmatic considerations. Rather, it will be stimulated and encouraged by God, each other, and all that's within us.

What will we discover in the New Jerusalem, a place of extravagant beauty and natural wonders? What awaits us as we explore the New Earth, a vast redeemed Eden, integrated with the best of human culture, under the reign of Christ?

Eternal Promises

Lift your eyes and look to the heavens:
    Who created all these?
He who brings out the starry host one by one,
    and calls them each by name.
Because of his great power and mighty strength,
    not one of them is missing.

ISAIAH 40:26

The heavens declare the glory of God;
    the skies proclaim the work of his hands.
Day after day they pour forth speech;
    night after night they display knowledge.
There is no speech or language
    where their voice is not heard.
Their voice goes out into all the earth,
    their words to the ends of the world.

PSALM 19:1-4

"Spectacular" Doesn't Begin to Describe It

Creatively speaking, God is just "warming up" in our universe.

On Mars, the volcano Olympus Mons rises 79,000 feet, nearly three times higher than Mount Everest, with a base that would cover the state of Nebraska. The Valles Marineris is a vast canyon that stretches one-sixth of the way around Mars. Hundreds of our Grand Canyons could fit inside it.

The New Earth may have far more spectacular features than these. Imagine what we might find on the new Mars or the new Saturn and Jupiter and their magnificent moons. I remember vividly the thrill of first seeing Saturn's rings through my new telescope when I was eleven years old. Five years later, I heard the gospel for the first time and came to know Jesus, but the wonders of the heavens helped lead me to God. How many times in the new universe will we be stunned by the awesomeness of God's creation?

Eternal Promises

My own hands stretched out the heavens;
    I marshaled their starry hosts.

ISAIAH 45:12

My own hand laid the foundations of the earth,
    and my right hand spread out the heavens;
when I summon them,
    they all stand up together.

ISAIAH 48:13

A Resurrected Universe

The Bible's final two chapters show that every aspect of the new creation will be greater than the old. Just as the present Jerusalem isn't nearly as great as the New Jerusalem, no part of the present creation—including the earth and the celestial heavens—is as great as it will be in the new creation.

While some passages suggest that the universe will wear out and the stars will be destroyed, others indicate that the stars will exist forever (Psalm 148:3-6). Is this a contradiction? No. We too will be destroyed by death, yet we will last forever. The earth will be destroyed in God's judgment, yet it will last forever. In exactly the same way, the stars will be destroyed, yet they will last forever. Based on the redemptive work of Christ, God will resurrect them.

Earth is the first domain of mankind's stewardship, but it is not the only domain. The entire new universe will be ours to travel to, inhabit, and rule—to God's glory.

Eternal Promises

He who began a good work in you will carry it on to completion until the day of Christ Jesus.

PHILIPPIANS 1:6

You have made known to me the path of life;
    you will fill me with joy in your presence,
        with eternal pleasures at your right hand.

PSALM 16:11

The Definitive Upgrade

Have you ever bought an economy ticket for a flight but because of overbooking or some other reason been upgraded to first class? Did you regret the upgrade? Did you spend your time wondering, *What am I missing out on by not being in the back of the plane?*

The upgrade from the old Earth to the New Earth will be vastly superior to that from economy to first class. (It may feel more like an upgrade to first class from the baggage hold.) Gone will be sin, the Curse, death, and suffering. In every way we will recognize that the New Earth is better—in no sense could it ever be worse.

If we would miss something from our old lives and the old Earth, it would be available to us on the New Earth. Why? Because we will experience all God intends for us. He fashions us to want precisely what he will give us, so what he gives us will be exactly what we want.

Eternal Promises

God saw all that he had made, and it was very good.

GENESIS 1:31

I praise you because I am fearfully and
    wonderfully made;
    your works are wonderful,
    I know that full well. . . .
When I was woven together in the depths
        of the earth,
    your eyes saw my unformed body.
All the days ordained for me
    were written in your book
    before one of them came to be.

PSALM 139:14-16

You, Only Better

God is the creator of individual identities and person-alities. He makes no two snowflakes, much less two people, alike. Not even "identical twins" are identical. Individuality preceded sin and the Curse. Individuality was God's plan from the beginning.

What makes you *you*? It's not only your body but also your memory, personality traits, gifts, passions, preferences, and interests. In the final resurrection, I believe all of these facets will be restored and ampli-fied, untarnished by sin and the Curse.

Do you remember a time when you really felt good about yourself? Not in pride or arrogance, but when you sensed you honored God, helped the needy, were faithful, humble, and servant-hearted, like Jesus? Do you remember when you encouraged someone? when you experienced who you were meant to be? when you were running or swimming or working and felt you were strong enough to go on forever (even though later you could hardly get out of bed)? That was a little taste of who you'll be in Heaven.

Eternal Promises

[Jesus said,] "I am the vine; you are the branches. If a man remains in me and I in him, he will bear much fruit."

JOHN 15:5

Be pure and blameless until the day of Christ, filled with the fruit of righteousness that comes through Jesus Christ—to the glory and praise of God.

PHILIPPIANS 1:10-11

The Garden Restored

Imagine a magnificent rose garden. It's been perfectly designed and cultivated. But the rosebushes become diseased. The garden becomes a tangled mass. It's a sad, deteriorated remnant of the glorious garden it once was. Then the gardener determines to reclaim his garden. Day after day he prunes, waters, and fertilizes each bush. His desire isn't simply to restore the garden to its original beauty; it's to make it far more beautiful than ever.

When the gardener is done and the roses are thriving and fragrant, is the rose garden the same as it was? Is each individual rose the same? Yes and no. It's the same rose garden, restored to its previous splendor and beyond. Yet to look at it, it's hard to believe these are the same roses that were once a withered, tangled mess.

This is a picture of Creation, Fall, and Resurrection. When God is finished, we'll be ourselves without the sin—meaning that we'll be the best we can be.

Eternal Promises

Ask now about the former days, long before your time,
from the day God created man on the earth; ask from
one end of the heavens to the other. Has anything so
great as this ever happened, or has anything like it ever
been heard of?

DEUTERONOMY 4:32

Ears that hear and eyes that see—
    the LORD has made them both.

PROVERBS 20:12

Heightened Senses

God designed us with five senses. They're part of what makes us human. Our resurrection bodies will surely have these senses. I expect they will increase in their power and sensitivity.

We'll stand on the New Earth and see its colors, feel its substance, smell its aromas, taste its fruits, and hear its sounds. Not figuratively. Literally. We know this because we're promised resurrection bodies like Christ's. He saw and heard and felt and, as he cooked and ate fish, he presumably smelled and tasted it (John 21:1-12). We will too.

Heaven's delights will stretch our glorified senses to their limits. How will things look, and how far away will we be able to see them? Will our eyes be able to function alternately as telescopes and microscopes? Will our ears serve as sound-gathering disks? Will our sense of smell be far more acute, able to identify a favorite flower—or person—miles away, so we can follow the scent to its source?

What God remakes, he only improves.

Eternal Promises

I pray also that the eyes of your heart may be enlightened in order that you may know the hope to which he has called you, the riches of his glorious inheritance in the saints.

EPHESIANS 1:18

Ascribe to the LORD, O families of nations,
     ascribe to the LORD glory and strength.
Ascribe to the LORD the glory due his name.

PSALM 96:7-8

God's Glory Displayed in Us

Have you heard it said of someone, "She's radiant"? I've met people so full of Jesus that they seem to have a physical brightness. If God himself shines in glory, then it seems appropriate that we, his image-bearers, will reflect his brightness. Now, moving beyond that analogy of our present condition, imagine people in the very presence of God, who are so righteous, so beautiful, so devoid of sin and darkness, so permeated by the very righteousness of God, that they have a literal physical radiance. That's not so hard to imagine, is it?

Shining speaks of glory, the outward display of greatness and majesty. *Glory* is a word associated with rulers. Kings had glory. We understandably hesitate to attribute glory to ourselves, but God doesn't hesitate to ascribe glory to us. As God's children we *should* bear his likeness. It's he, not we, who declares that we are royalty—kings and queens who will reign with Christ.

Eternal Promises

[Jesus said,] "Let the little children come to me, and do not hinder them, for the kingdom of God belongs to such as these."

MARK 10:14

[Jesus] said to them, "Whoever welcomes this little child in my name welcomes me; and whoever welcomes me welcomes the one who sent me. For he who is least among you all—he is the greatest."

LUKE 9:48

Like a Child

The New Earth will be a place of both maturity and perfection. Regardless of what age we appear, I believe that our bodies will demonstrate the qualities of youthfulness that Jesus so valued in children. God put special qualities into children, ones we—and he—delight in. I fully expect all of us to have such qualities as curiosity, gratefulness, longing to learn and explore, and eagerness to hear stories and gather close to loved ones.

We'll be unburdened by the Curse that shrivels not just our bodies but also our spirits, robbing many of youthfulness. Jonathan Edwards stated, "The heavenly inhabitants . . . remain in eternal youth."[8] Heaven will be full of children . . . even if we look like adults. What we love about children is their joy, exuberance, curiosity, laughter, and spontaneity. In Heaven, whether or not anyone is the size and appearance of a child, we'll all be childlike in the ways that will bring joy to us and to our Father.

Eternal Promises

By a single offering [Jesus] has perfected for all time those who are being sanctified.

HEBREWS 10:14, ESV

[All] are justified freely by his grace through the redemption that came by Christ Jesus. God presented him as a sacrifice of atonement, through faith in his blood.

ROMANS 3:24-25

Sin's Final Defeat

Christ promises on the New Earth, "There will be no more death or mourning or crying or pain, for the old order of things has passed away" (Revelation 21:4). Since "the wages of sin is death" (Romans 6:23), the promise of no more death is a promise of *no more sin*. Those who will never die can never sin, since sinners always die. Sin causes mourning, crying, and pain. If those will never occur again, then *sin* can never occur again.

Scripture emphasizes that Christ died *once* to deal with sin and will never again need to die (Hebrews 9:26-28; 10:10; 1 Peter 3:18). We'll have the very righteousness of God (2 Corinthians 5:21). We won't sin in Heaven for the same reason God doesn't: He cannot sin. Our eternal inability to sin has been purchased by Christ's blood.

On the cross, validated by his resurrection, our Savior purchased our perfection *for all time*.

Eternal Promises

Christ was sacrificed once to take away the sins of many people; and he will appear a second time, not to bear sin, but to bring salvation to those who are waiting for him.

HEBREWS 9:28

Christ died for sins once for all, the righteous for the unrighteous, to bring you to God. He was put to death in the body but made alive by the Spirit.

1 PETER 3:18

Free at Last

What's the hope we should live for? It's more than freedom from suffering. It's deliverance from *sin*, freeing us to be fully human. Paul says, "In this hope we were saved" (Romans 8:24). What hope? The words of the previous verse tell us: "the redemption of our bodies" (v. 23). That's the final resurrection, when death will be swallowed up and sin will be reversed, never again to touch us. This is what we should long for and live for. Resurrection will mean many things—including *no more sin*.

   Is resurrected living in a resurrected world with the resurrected Christ and his resurrected people *your* daily longing and hope? Is it part of the gospel you share with others? In liberating us from sin and all its consequences, the Resurrection will free us to live with God, gaze on him, and enjoy his uninterrupted fellowship forever, with no threat that anything will ever again come between us and him.

Eternal Promises

The King will say . . . , "Come, you who are blessed by my Father; take your inheritance, the kingdom prepared for you since the creation of the world. For I was hungry and you gave me something to eat, I was thirsty and you gave me something to drink, I was a stranger and you invited me in."

MATTHEW 25:34-35

Sell your possessions and give to the poor. Provide purses for yourselves that will not wear out, a treasure in heaven that will not be exhausted, where no thief comes near and no moth destroys.

LUKE 12:33

Rewarded for Acts of Kindness

How many times have we done small acts of kindness on Earth without realizing the effects? How many times have we shared Christ with people we thought didn't take it to heart but who years later came to Jesus partly because of the seeds we planted? How many times have we spoken up for unborn children and seen no result, but as a result someone chose not to have an abortion and saved a child's life? How many dishes have been washed and diapers changed and crying children sung to in the middle of the night, when we couldn't see the impact of the love we showed? And how many times have we seen no response, but God was still pleased by our efforts?

God *is* watching. He *is* keeping track. In Heaven he'll reward us for our acts of faithfulness to him, right down to every cup of cold water we've given to the needy in his name (Mark 9:41). And he's making a permanent record in Heaven's books.

Eternal Promises

From one man [God] made every nation of men, that they should inhabit the whole earth; and he determined the times set for them and the exact places where they should live.

ACTS 17:26

How can we thank God enough for you in return for all the joy we have in the presence of our God because of you?

1 THESSALONIANS 3:9

Divinely Appointed Coincidence

Do you have a close friend who's had a profound influence on you? Do you think it is a coincidence that she was in your dorm wing or became your roommate? Was it accidental that your desk was near hers or that his family lived next door or that your father was transferred when you were in third grade so that you ended up in her neighborhood? God orchestrates our lives.

Since God determined the time and exact places you would live, it's no accident which neighborhood you grew up in, who lived next door, who went to school with you, who was part of your church youth group, who was there to help you and pray for you. Our relationships were appointed by God, and there's every reason to believe those relationships will continue in Heaven.

God's plan doesn't stop on the New Earth; it continues. God doesn't abandon his purposes; he extends and fulfills them. Friendships begun on Earth will continue in Heaven, getting richer than ever.

Eternal Promises

Peter said to him, "We have left everything to follow you!" "I tell you the truth," Jesus replied, "no one who has left home or brothers or sisters or mother or father or children or fields for me and the gospel will fail to receive a hundred times as much in this present age (homes, brothers, sisters, mothers, children and fields—and with them, persecutions) and in the age to come, eternal life."

MARK 10:28-30

God so loved the world that he gave his one and only Son, that whoever believes in him shall not perish but have eternal life.

JOHN 3:16

Life as It Is Meant to Be Lived

If you're a child of God, you do *not* just "go around once" on Earth. You don't get just one earthly life. You get another—one far better and without end. You'll inhabit the New Earth! You'll live with the God you cherish and the people you love as an undying person on an undying Earth. Those who go to Hell are the ones who go around only once on this earth.

We use the term *eternal life* without thinking what it means. *Life* is an earthly existence in which we work, rest, play, and relate to each other in ways that include the cultivation and enjoyment of culture. Yet we have redefined *eternal life* to mean an off-Earth existence stripped of the defining properties of what we know life to be. Eternal life will be enjoying forever what life on Earth is at its finest moments, what it was intended to be.

Eternal Promises

God raised us up with Christ and seated us with him in the heavenly realms in Christ Jesus, in order that in the coming ages he might show the incomparable riches of his grace, expressed in his kindness to us in Christ Jesus.

EPHESIANS 2:6-7

Joyfully [give] thanks to the Father, who has qualified you to share in the inheritance of the saints in the kingdom of light.

COLOSSIANS 1:11-12

The Best Is Yet to Come

One day we'll all have bodies and minds far better than the best we ever knew here. We'll converse with a brilliance and wit and joy and strength we've never known.

I don't look back nostalgically at wonderful moments in my life, wistfully thinking the best days are behind me. I look at them as foretastes of an eternity of better things. The buds of this life's greatest moments don't shrivel and die; they blossom into greater moments, each to be treasured, none to be lost. Everything done in dependence on God will bear fruit for eternity. This life need not be wasted. In small and often unnoticed acts of service to Christ, we can invest this life in eternity, where today's faithfulness will forever pay rich dividends.

"Thanks, Lord, that the best is yet to be." That's my prayer. God will one day clear away sin, death, and sorrow, as surely as builders clear away debris so they can begin new construction.

Eternal Promises

Your Father has been pleased to give you the kingdom.

LUKE 12:32

[A loud voice from the throne said,] "He will wipe every tear from their eyes. There will be no more death or mourning or crying or pain, for the old order of things has passed away." He who was seated on the throne said, "I am making everything new!" Then he said, "Write this down, for these words are trustworthy and true."

REVELATION 21:4-5

The Adventure Can Be Yours

> I saw a new heaven and a new earth. . . . And
> I heard a loud voice from the throne saying,
> "Now the dwelling of God is with men, and
> he will live with them. They will be his people,
> and God himself will be with them and be their
> God." (Revelation 21:1, 3)

These are the words of King Jesus. Count on them.
Live every day in light of them. Make every choice in
light of Christ's certain promise.

We were all made for a person and a place. Jesus is
the person. Heaven is the place.

If you know Jesus, I'll join you in that resurrected
world. With the Lord we love and with the friends we
cherish, we'll embark on the ultimate adventure, in a
spectacular new universe awaiting our exploration and
dominion. Jesus will be the center of all things, and joy
will be the air we breathe.

NOTES

1. Charles H. Spurgeon, *Morning and Evening*, April 25, morning reading.

2. Gerhard Kittel and Gerhard Friedrich, eds., Geoffrey W. Bromiley, trans. and ed., *Theological Dictionary of the New Testament* (Grand Rapids: Eerdmans, 1964–76), 2:288.

3. "Sight Unseen," *World* (November 8, 2003): 13; see the article "One Unseen Divinity? Ridiculous! Billions of Unseen Universes? Sure, Why Not?" discussed at "Easterblogg," The New Republic Online, http://www.tnr.com/easterbrook .mhtml?week=2003-10-21.53.

4. Peter Toon, *Heaven and Hell: A Biblical and Theological Overview* (Nashville: Nelson, 1986), 26.

5. The Westminster Shorter Catechism may be viewed online: "Westminster Shorter Catechism with Proof Texts," Center for Reformed Theology and Apologetics, http:// www.reformed.org/documents/WSC_frames.html?wsc_ text=WSC.html.

6. Maltbie D. Babcock, "This Is My Father's World," 1901.

7. J. Boudreau, *The Happiness of Heaven* (Rockford, IL: Tan Books, 1984), 95–96.

8. Jonathan Edwards, quoted in John Gerstner, *Jonathan Edwards on Heaven and Hell* (Grand Rapids: Baker, 1980), 39.

SCRIPTURE INDEX

ABOUT THE AUTHOR

Randy Alcorn is the founder of Eternal Perspective Ministries (EPM). Prior to starting EPM, he served as a pastor for fourteen years. He has spoken around the world and has taught at Multnomah Bible College and Western Seminary in Portland, Oregon.

Randy is the bestselling author of more than forty books (with five million copies in print), including the novels *Deadline, Dominion, Deception, The Ishbane Conspiracy, Safely Home,* and *Courageous.* His nonfiction works include *Heaven; If God Is Good; Managing God's Money; Money, Possessions, and Eternity; The Treasure Principle; The Grace and Truth Paradox;* and *The Law of Rewards.* Randy has written for many magazines, including EPM's *Eternal Perspectives.*

He is active daily on Facebook and Twitter and has been a guest on more than 700 radio, television, and online programs, including *Focus on the Family, FamilyLife Today, Revive Our Hearts, The Bible Answer Man,* and the Resurgence.

The father of two married daughters, Karina and Angela, Randy lives in Gresham, Oregon, with his wife and best friend, Nanci. They are the proud grandparents of five grandchildren.

Follow Randy on Facebook:
www.facebook.com/randyalcorn

Twitter: www.twitter.com/randyalcorn

Blog: www.epm.org/blog

OTHER BOOKS BY RANDY ALCORN

FICTION

Deadline
Dominion
Deception
Edge of Eternity
Lord Foulgrin's Letters
The Ishbane Conspiracy
Safely Home
Courageous
The Chasm

NONFICTION

Heaven
Touchpoints: Heaven
50 Days of Heaven
In Light of Eternity
Managing God's Money
Money, Possessions, and Eternity
The Law of Rewards
ProLife Answers to ProChoice Arguments
Sexual Temptation: Guardrails for the Road to Purity
The Goodness of God
The Grace and Truth Paradox
The Purity Principle
The Treasure Principle
Why ProLife?
If God Is Good
The Promise of Heaven
We Shall See God
90 Days of God's Goodness
Life Promises for Eternity
Eternal Perspectives

KIDS

Heaven for Kids
Wait until Then
Tell Me about Heaven